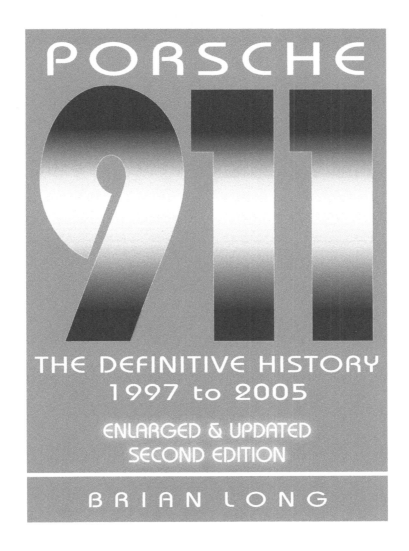

PORSCHE 911

THE DEFINITIVE HISTORY
1997 to 2005

ENLARGED & UPDATED
SECOND EDITION

BRIAN LONG

T0386647

VELOCE PUBLISHING
THE PUBLISHER OF FINE AUTOMOTIVE BOOKS

Other books from Veloce –

General Porsche
Cranswick on Porsche (Cranswick)
Porsche Boxster (Long)
Porsche 356 (2nd Edition) (Long)
Porsche 908 (Födisch, Neßhöver, Roßbach, Schwarz & Roßbach)
Porsche 911 Carrera – The Last of the Evolution (Corlett)
Porsche 911R, RS & RSR, 4th Edition (Starkey)
Porsche 911 – The Definitive History 1963-1971 (Long)
Porsche 911 – The Definitive History 1971-1977 (Long)
Porsche 911 – The Definitive History 1977-1987 (Long)
Porsche 911 – The Definitive History 1987-1997 (Long)
Porsche 911 – The Definitive History 1997-2004 (Long)
Porsche 911 – The Definitive History 2004-2012 (Long)
Porsche 911, The Book of the Air-Cooled – Limited Edition (Long)
Porsche 911 SC – Experiences & illustrated practical advice from one man's home restoration (Clusker)
Porsche 911SC 'Super Carrera' – The Essential Companion (Streather)
Porsche 914 & 914-6: The Definitive History of the Road & Competition Cars (Long)
Porsche - The Racing 914s – (Smith)
Porsche 924 Carrera, The (Smith)
Porsche 924 (Long)
Porsche 928 (Long)
Porsche 944 (Long)
Porsche 964, 993 & 996 Data Plate Code Breaker (Streather)
Porsche 993 'King Of Porsche' – The Essential Companion (Streather)
Porsche 996 'Supreme Porsche' – The Essential Companion (Streather)
Porsche 997 'Porsche Excellence – The Essential Companion (Streather)
Porsche Racing Cars – 1953 to 1975 (Long)
Porsche Racing Cars – 1976 to 2005 (Long)
Porsche - Silver Steeds (Smith)
Porsche – The Rally Story (Meredith)

Essential Buyer's Guide Series
Porsche 356 (Johnson)
Porsche 911SC (Streather)
Porsche 911 Carrera 3.2 (Streather)
Porsche 911 (993) (Streather)
Porsche 911 (964) (Streather)
Porsche 911 (996) (Streather)
Porsche 911 (997) – Model years 2004 to 2009 (Streather)
Porsche 911 (997) – Second generation models 2009 to 2012 (Streather)
Porsche 924 – All models 1976 to 1988 (Hodgkins)
Porsche 928 (Hemmings)
Porsche 930 Turbo & 911 (930) Turbo (Streather)
Porsche 944 (Higgins)
Porsche 981 Boxster & Cayman (Streather)
Porsche 986 Boxster (Streather)
Porsche 987 Boxster & Cayman (Streather)

Veloce's other imprints:

www.veloce.co.uk

First published in 2005, second edition published in March 2017, this Veloce Classic Reprint published June 2019 by Veloce Publishing Limited, Veloce House, Parkway Farm Business Park, Middle Farm Way, Poundbury, Dorchester, Dorset, DT1 3AR, England. Fax 01305 250479/Tel 01305 260068/e-mail info@veloce.co.uk/web www.veloce.co.uk or www.velocebooks.com.. ISBN: 978-1-787115-51-4; UPC: 6-36847-01551-0.

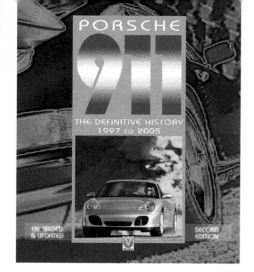

CONTENTS

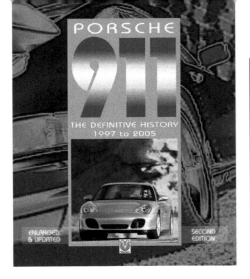

Introduction & Acknowledgements

INTRODUCTION

The 996 was the first of the water-cooled 911s, breaking the use of air-cooled engines for this signature Porsche sports car – a tradition that had lasted over three decades. Having made the break, though, the model was subjected to a programme of continuous development and allowed to evolve in a typically Porsche way, with increasingly sportier versions following year after year to keep this classic machine ahead of the competition.

This volume now takes the 911 story from its origins, through the prototype stages and on to 2005, the year that signalled the end of the 996 series, taking a look at the car's racing exploits along the way. The book is full of contemporary factory-sourced images and detailed information on the cars sold in all the major markets around the world, thus providing the perfect guide for enthusiasts, historians and those looking for authenticity.

ACKNOWLEDGEMENTS

My original book on the first of the water-cooled Porsche 911s was published in 2005 as part of a five-volume set (now six), with help coming from Klaus Parr, Jens Torner and Dieter Gross at Porsche, Family Garage and K3 Works (now Nobel Co. Limited) in Chiba, Kenichi Kobayashi at Miki Press, and the Japan Motor Industry Federation library in Tokyo.

The reality is, very little has changed. Now Klaus has retired, even though we stay in touch, it is poor Jens that deals with my numerous requests – as he has done, without a single complaint, for more years than either of us would care to remember. Our shared love of photography and the Kawasaki brand keeps our relationship alive in much the same way as the one between myself and his former boss – we are friends first and foremost, and will remain so long after I've written my last book. My sincere thanks, as always, to some of the best people in the business.

Brian Long
Chiba City, Japan

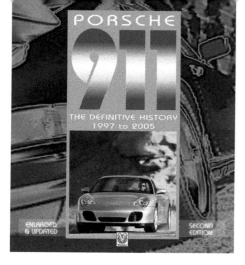

1

A brief history of Porsche

If one utters the word 'Porsche,' there is an immediate association with quality of engineering, innovation, and probably speed. When one looks at the foundation of the brand, perhaps it's not so surprising ...

Professor Ferdinand Porsche had worked for Lohner, Austro-Daimler, Daimler (which soon after became Daimler-Benz) and Steyr, and had an unrivalled reputation in Germany as a designer.

After leaving the latter concern, he felt the time had come to establish his own company. Registered in April 1931, a design studio was set up in Stuttgart with a team of handpicked engineers and designers. This team included Porsche's son, Ferry, who was then just 21 years old.

Ferry Porsche inherited much of his father's natural flair for

Early Volkswagen prototypes outside the Porsche family home in Stuttgart.

engineering and, although he wanted to become a racing driver, his father soon put a stop to his aspirations. This is perhaps fortunate for, without him, the Porsche company, as it exists today, would never have evolved, and neither would the vehicles recognized as 'true' Porsches.

As Germany's Chancellor, Adolf Hitler was naturally very supportive of German industry, and financed the Mercedes-Benz and Auto Union racing programmes to show the world the strength of German engineering. The highly successful Auto Union V16 Grand Prix car was a Porsche design, of course, but it was the Volkswagen project which provided the basis for the Porsche success story. The Volkswagen was also financed by the Nazi Party – a blessing at the time which caused problems later.

Just as Hitler was passing the final plans for the Volkswagen, the Second World War broke out. During the hostilities, Porsche and his team were moved to the Austrian village of Gmünd, and there they produced many designs, including those for a number of tanks. Because of his 'links' with the Nazi leader, Professor Porsche was arrested and interrogated by the Allied authorities following the war, but was promptly released. He went to Renault and, whilst there, Porsche and his son-in-law were arrested and imprisioned by the French on war criminal charges, with a ransom of one million francs. (Ferry Porsche had also been imprisoned for a short time, but his sister had managed to negotiate his release.)

However, the Porsche offices in Stuttgart were occupied by the United States Army, and Ferry Porsche had little chance of raising the ransom money by repairing ex-Army Volkswagens. By an amazing stroke of luck, Porsche was approached by Carlo Abarth (the famous engine tuner) and Piero Dusio, a rich Italian industrialist who, among other things, wanted to build a Grand Prix car.

The Cisitalia, as it was known, drew heavily on prewar Auto Union designs, and was very complex. Sadly, the project was destined to fail, as escalating costs put a potentially successful car out of reach of even Dusio's wealth. It did, however, provide Ferry Porsche with enough money to free his father, and the Professor was allowed back to Austria in August 1947, but died less than four years later. His health had never been the

Ferry Porsche (left) and his father pictured with Porsche Number One. While this roadster was mid-engined, the closed car that followed adopted the traditional VW rear-engined layout, with the gearbox and transaxle in front of the powerplant. For many years this was a key feature of the Porsche road car line.

This Beutler-bodied cabriolet was one of six produced by the Swiss coachbuilder, based on the Gmünd chassis.

European Grand Prix in Switzerland to allow journalists to try the car, and it was at this meeting that Porsche met Rupprecht von Senger, who was particularly enthusiastic. Von Senger and his partner agreed to buy the next four cars, and also proved very helpful in getting supplies from Wolfsburg to Gmünd.

The second car was a coupé, completed in July 1948. Aerodynamics were very good and, combined with the lack of openings at the front and the seamless construction of the body, meant the Porsche was capable of some very high speeds for such a small-engined car.

same following his imprisonment, but at least he was able to see his son develop a new car bearing the family name.

The legendary 356

Design work on the Type 356 sports car had begun in Gmünd after Ferry Porsche decided that his small company should construct a vehicle based on Volkswagen components. Fortunately, the British had managed to revive the VW factory after the war, and the first drawing was dated 17 July 1947, just one month after the project was instigated.

The first chassis was completed in March 1948, and fitted with a prototype open body two months later. The spaceframe chassis on Number One was well designed, but unsuitable for cost-effective series production as it was very labour-intensive to build.

The engine was a tuned 1131cc Volkswagen unit, mounted back to front to give good weight distribution, which, unfortunately, took up too much space to allow for any more than two seats. A number of other problems were encountered with this setup and, from the second car, the engine was mounted in traditional Volkswagen fashion on a sheet steel platform chassis.

Number One was taken to the

A couple of Gmünd coupés photographed in France. Note the bumper mounted on the body and the split windscreen. The 356 quickly established itself in competition; interestingly, the works always used the alloy Gmünd coupés, as they were lighter than the Stuttgart-built machines.

Announced during the summer of 1948, the car's public debut was scheduled for the Geneva Show in 1949. It wasn't long before a 1086cc capacity was chosen, allowing the cars to compete in the 1100cc Class at international level. In the meantime, in mid-September 1948, Porsche sealed a deal with Volkswagen securing the supply of parts (VW was now back in German hands, headed by the capable Heinz Nordhoff), as well as the use of the Volkswagen dealer and service network.

The Gmünd cars were completely handbuilt, their aluminium bodies beaten into shape, as there simply wasn't the money available to tool up. According to Ferry Porsche, 46 cars were built at Gmünd between June 1948 and March 1951. However, figures vary wildly between sources, with most quoting 50 or 51 vehicles.

Serious production began early in 1950 when the firm moved back to Stuttgart. The Porsche site was still being used by the Americans at the time, so the factory belonging to Porsche's neighbour – the Reutter body works – was used initially. Reutter had already been given the contract to build new steel bodies for Porsche in November 1949, and an area was set aside for the motor manufacturer.

The first steel-bodied Porsche was completed in April 1950. There were a number of small differences to the Gmünd alloy cars, but they were indeed subtle. In fact, mild and constant updating was to become a feature of Porsche production through the years, the company preferring to introduce new models that were evolutions of the outgoing vehicle. Even competition Porsches were largely based on production cars during these early days.

At the 1950 Paris Show, an ailing Ferdinand Porsche held talks with Max Hoffman and others to try and get the 356 into America. By the end of 1950, he was gravely ill, and died a national hero in January 1951.

In the meantime, in December 1950, a small design and management office was purchased near the Reutter works, and a racing shop was attached with just enough room for two cars and four mechanics. It was at this stage in the proceedings that the company was registered as Dr Ing. h. c. F. Porsche KG. The Stuttgart concern had a staff of 108, with planned production of around ten cars per month. In the event, this target was easily doubled, and nearly 300 Porsche 356s were built in the year. The 500th German-built 356 was driven out of the works in March 1951, and just five months later the 1000th 356 left the factory.

By March 1951, 1283cc engines were available, and a 1488cc unit followed in October. Although the 1100 engine continued until the end of 1954, there were fewer sales of the smaller capacity models, especially in America, a market which was already very important to the company.

In September 1952, the 1500 gave a refined 55bhp, while the roller bearing engine – giving 70bhp – became known as the 1500 Super. Other important revisions carried out during 1952 included dropping the old two-piece windscreen, although the distinct V-shape remained until 1955. Stronger bumpers, now moved further away from the body, were also a feature.

The original Porsche factory was supposed to have been handed back in September 1950 but, due to the alert caused by the Korean War, the American authorities held on to it.

8

With no sign of the old factory being returned, another works was built in 1952, next door to Reutter. By November 1952, the first cars were starting to roll out of Werk II.

From November 1953, a roller bearing version of the 1300 was made available and called the 1300 Super. Launched at the Paris Salon, this 60bhp unit was shortlived, remaining in production for only six months; all pushrod roller bearing engines were phased out by the end of 1957.

Dr Ernst Fuhrmann began designing the powerful Carrera engine during 1952. In order to keep its size down, he devised an ingenious system incorporating no fewer than nine shafts, fourteen bevel gears and two spur gears to operate the dohc per bank arrangement. The beauty of this system was that the engine's overall dimensions were little changed from the standard unit. The first engine was up and running in April 1953 – it was right virtually from the start, and testing took place in the new Porsche 550 at the Nürburgring in August.

A Carrera engine was installed in one of the works Gmünd coupés, and entered for the 1954 Liège-Rome-Liège Rally, held that particular year in August. Ferry Porsche's theory was that if the unit could survive such a tough event, it could safely be put into a production car: the decision was made easier after Herbert Linge and Helmut Polensky won outright.

In 1954, the staff increased to 493, but only 1934 cars were produced – 44 less than in the previous year. However, on 15 March 1954, the 5000th German-built Porsche was constructed (two years later the figure reached 10,000) and exports now accounted for 60 per cent of production. Interestingly, VW in Wolfsburg was by now employing over 20,000 people to make an average of 670 cars a day, and in August 1955, the one millionth Beetle was produced.

John von Neumann, Porsche's West Coast distributor, was the inspiration behind the Speedster. The Speedster was exactly what Hoffman needed to boost sales Stateside, selling at $2995 in basic form. Based on the Cabriolet but with minimal equipment, such as a cheap hood, a low and flimsy windscreen, and detachable side-screens instead of wind-up windows, it was introduced into America in September 1954. In all, a total of 4854 Speedsters were produced (both 356 and 356A types together), and it became the darling of the racing set.

At the 1951 Earls Court Show, two Porsche 356s – a coupé and a cabriolet – were put on display by Connaught Cars Ltd, becoming the first German cars to be shown in England since the end of the war. Before long, AFN Ltd of Isleworth (the concern behind Frazer-Nash) became an agent, with imports starting seriously in 1954. Prices ranged from £1842 to £2378, which was quite expensive considering that a Jaguar XK120 was around £1600 at this time, and the almost unlimited choice of even cheaper British sports cars.

The 356A was introduced at the Frankfurt Show in September 1955. There were subtle changes to the body, and suspension improvements made the car feel more stable going into corners. The 356s were still being used successfully in rallying with the Liège-Rome-Liège becoming a Porsche benefit. The racing side of competition was left almost exclusively to the Spyders, although there were Class

Delightful period shot of a 356A coupé with American-style bumper guards.

wins on both the Mille Miglia and Targa Florio.

The 1582cc engine arrived in 1955 in two guises; the 1600 and 1600 Super giving 60bhp and 75bhp respectively. The 1300 and 1300 Super continued unchanged in most markets, but had been dropped in America earlier in the year and were phased out completely by the end of 1957. The 1500GS Carrera engine was made available for the new 356A range and, like the other power units, could be specified in the updated coupé, cabriolet or Speedster bodyshells.

On 1 December 1955, the old works was at last handed back to its rightful owner. Called Werk I, the management, along with the Design, Experimental, and Racing Departments moved there, as did the Repair Shop. Towards the end of 1955, three out of every four cars produced by Porsche (which by now employed around 600 people) was exported, the majority finding their way to America.

There were fewer changes to the cars now as production increased; teardrop tail lights replaced the twin round ones in March 1957, but by far the biggest changes came when the T-2 body was introduced at the 1957 Frankfurt Show. Following the Show, the Carrera became available in two versions – a De Luxe (GS) model with different carburation and an improved heater, and the GT. The 110bhp GT was available only as a Speedster or coupé intended mainly for competition.

In August 1958 the Speedster was superceded by the Convertible D (the D added in recognition of the coachbuilder Drauz of Heilbronn) with a more serviceable hood, a better windscreen, padded seats and wind-up side windows: much more in line with Ferry Porsche's ideals.

Porsche in competition
Based on the original Porsche Number One, the Type 550 made its debut in May 1953 for the Eifelrennen at the Nürburgring. On this occasion, the mid-engined car was powered by a 1500 Super unit and narrowly beat the Borgwards to take a maiden Class victory. It provided the Porsche concern with the foundation stone on which to build a racing legend.

By the early part of 1954, the first of the customer cars were being completed by Wendler of Reutlingen. The 1500 Super engine was used, but tuned to bring power up to around 100bhp. The official designation was 550/1500RS, but Max Hoffman coined the name 'Spyder,' and it was this that stuck in the public's mind.

Excellent results at Le Mans, on the Carrera Panamericana, the Mille Miglia (the 1954 event was the international debut of the 550 Spyder with the Carrera engine), the Tour de France Automobile, Tourist Trophy, and numerous tracks across Europe and America secured the Spyder a place in racing history.

The Wendler-bodied 550A had been introduced in April 1956. Gone was the ladder chassis of the old Spyder, replaced by a lighter but stiffer spaceframe, and it incorporated a low pivot swing axle rear suspension. The 550A gave Porsche its first taste of victory on the Targa Florio, and there were many Class wins.

The Type 718 prototype was built up over the winter of 1956/57. Based on the one-off Type 645, it was a lighter machine again, built around a spaceframe chassis, and was some 125mm (5in) lower than the old 550 Spyder. An improved suspension, superior braking and 142bhp resulted in a far better car. The mid-engined 718 RS became the 718 RSK through further suspension changes – these were later changed back, but the RSK name stayed.

Formula Two returned in 1957, the new regulations dictating that 1.5-litre engines running on pump fuel would form the basis for the series. Porsche entered a couple of races, and actually won the F2 Class at the Nürburgring Grand Prix with a 550A.

The RSK made only two appearances at the race track in the 1957 season, but, by the early part of 1958, the definitive 718 RSK had arrived. On the 1959 Targa Florio, Edgar Barth and Wolfgang Seidel took Porsche's second victory on the classic

A short stop on the 1953 Carrera Panamericana. The marque's success in this event led to the 'Carrera' name being adopted on a number of later high performance models.

11

The 550A Spyder photographed at the works.

event, followed home by three other Porsche drivers.

As early as 1953, Ferry Porsche had hinted that Porsche may become involved in Grand Prix racing. During October 1958, the CSI announced that Formula One would run with 1.5-litre cars with a minimum weight of 500kg for 1961 – the rules seemed ideally suited to Porsche. In the meantime, the company continued to field the RSK in Formula Two races. A programme was instigated so that Porsche would have an open-wheeled F2 car for 1959, using it as a test-bed for the proposed F1 machine for 1961. It was running by April 1959, and was very much the same as the Type 718 under the skin, save for the new narrow chassis frame, and the detail changes that this necessitated.

The car was improved as the season progressed, and Stirling Moss was impressed enough to test it, with the result that Rob Walker was loaned one of the new works F2 cars for Moss' use during the 1960 season. Porsche won the 1960 Formula Two Championship.

The company's F1 debut came at Brussels on 9 April 1961, but the cars consistently failed to achieve the desired results. Dan Gurney's victory in the 1962 French Grand Prix was Porsche's only win in a World Championship event. Formula One proved too expensive, and, despite having invested a small fortune in developing the flat-eight engine, Porsche decided to cut its losses and withdraw gracefully from the Grand Prix arena.

To tackle the ever-increasing threat from Alfa Romeo and Lotus, Porsche exploited the FIA rules to the limit, and had a new Carrera made ready to retain its position at the top of the 1600 Class. 25 chassis were reserved by Porsche for the Abarth-Carrera project, although, eventually, only 20 of the lightweight Zagato-bodied cars were built. Four or five were made ready for works drivers in 1960: Class wins came at Le Mans, on the Targa Florio, at Sebring, and the Nürburgring.

The RS60 had a larger windscreen than the old RSK to comply with new FIA regulations for 1960. Otherwise, the RS60 was basically similar to the

Paul Strahle hustling the Abarth-Carrera on the 1962 Targa Florio.

718, except for the slightly longer wheelbase and more powerful engine. The similar-looking RS61 followed for the 1961 season.

356 developments

The 356B made its public debut at the 1959 Frankfurt Show, distinguished by the higher position of the headlights in a new wing line, and higher and stronger bumpers. The standard 1.6-litre 60bhp engine of the 356A was retained, as was the Super, but this was now known as the Super 75 to differentiate it from the new Super 90. This 90bhp unit was available from March 1960, and was considered powerful enough to render the Carrera model unnecessary. For the time being at least, a Carrera was not listed.

The 356B was initially catalogued with three body styles: the Convertible D was renamed the Roadster, and the coupé and cabriolet made up the range. In August 1960, they were joined by the short-lived Karmann hardtop coupé. A third factory (Werk III) had been built at Zuffenhausen toward the end of 1959 to cope with the workload, and by 1960 turnover was around 90,000,000 DM a year.

At the Frankfurt Show in September 1961, the T-6 body made its debut. A number of new features distinguished the latest model, such as the larger front and rear windows on the coupé, a new engine cover with two grilles fitted across the range, and a larger front hood featuring a squarer-shaped leading edge (which gave more luggage space).

At the same time as the T-6 356B was introduced, the Carrera returned to the line-up. Named the Carrera 2, it had a two-litre version of the Carrera engine, and was sold to the public from the following April. The Carrera 2 introduced disc brakes to the Porsche marque for the first time, and with 130bhp on tap, a top speed of 124mph (200kph) was possible. The 50,000th German-built Porsche left the line in April 1962, but shortly afterward the Karmann hardtop coupé and the Roadster were discontinued due to falling sales.

Introduced in July 1963, the 356C was basically a stopgap model until the new 911 became established. More refined than its predecessors, the body was very much the same as that of the 356B (offered in coupé and cabriolet forms, with the option of a detachable steel hardtop for the latter); the main changes were mechanical.

There were new 75bhp and 95bhp engines, a modified rear suspension, and disc brakes were standard across the range. However, the basic layout of

Among other things, the 356B brought a new wing line, and revised bumpers and lighting arrangements, all clearly visible in this photograph taken during an interview with Ferry Porsche in 1960.

The 356C, seen here at Schloss Solitude in cabriolet guise, had a similar body to the last of the 356Bs. The 356C was short-lived by Porsche standards, as the 911 and 912 were waiting in the wings.

four air-cooled cylinders, horizontally opposed in pairs, remained unchanged throughout the 17 year lifespan of the 356. The body changed little, but all the time was being brought up-to-date, regularly acquiring features tested in the field of motorsport.

Porsche intended that a white cabriolet completed in September 1965 would be the last 356, and it was, officially. But then the Dutch Police placed a special order for ten vehicles in 1966, which were initiated in March. The total number of 356s built came to 76,313.

Despite the demand for the 356, it was obvious that the model wasn't going to last forever, and Porsche began to prepare for its ultimate replacement in the late fifties. Ferry Porsche wanted the new car to be slightly bigger and a true 2+2. The Type 695 project began in 1959, but was later rejected in favour of a new coupé design from Butzi Porsche – the Type 901.

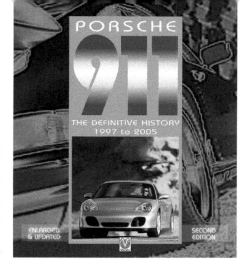

2

The early
911 models

While the Porsche marque has exceptional bloodlines at the heart of its foundation, more than any other model, it was probably the 911 that established it as a world player.

The 356 was never going to be an easy vehicle to replace. It had a fanatical following that few other cars enjoyed, and the long production life of the series meant it was synonymous with the Porsche name. The racers came and went, but the 356 continued year after year as an ambassador of the marque. However, it was obvious that the 356 could not go on forever – a new car was needed to take Porsche into a new era.

The 1963 Frankfurt Show saw the debut of the 901, the very machine that would carry the torch for the German company in the future, but its appearance was somewhat premature. At least the leading features of the 901 gave a good idea of what enthusiasts could expect to see in the showrooms in the coming seasons.

In its report on the premier

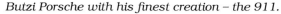

Butzi Porsche with his finest creation – the 911.

One of the early styling proposals put forward under the Type 695 study. Following on from this, work on the Type 754 body (T-7) duly began in late 1959, ultimately giving rise to the T-8 coupé – origin of the 911 series.

A rare view of the styling studio at the time of the 911's initial development stage. Butzi Porsche can be seen to the right; note also the 904 models in the background.

German motor show, *MotorSport* observed: "The car on the stand at Frankfurt was 'the only one we've got' or words to that effect, and as they have no intention of making any for at least a year one wonders why they didn't wait until the next Frankfurt Show to introduce it, unless it was to forestall the more sensationally minded continental newspapers.

"However, its specification is interesting for it uses an intriguing new flat-six air-cooled engine of two-litre capacity with single overhead chain-driven camshafts for each bank which gives 130bhp (DIN) at 6200rpm. The new engine, which uses an eight main bearing crankshaft and is, of course, the first Porsche to eschew gear-driven camshafts, is mated to an all-new five-speed gearbox/final-drive unit.

"The car is not a full four-seater but the two occasional rear seats should remain comfortable for a little longer than the usual 'legless dwarf' variety. The car itself remains unmistakably a Porsche in appearance except for its longer wheelbase and different front and rear end styling.

"The front suspension is similar to the MacPherson principle except that torsion bars are used as the springing medium, while the rear suspension retains trailing arms and transverse torsion bars. Disc brakes of Porsche/Ate construction are fitted on all wheels.

"Porsche claim a top speed of 120mph [192kph] and a standing start quarter-mile in 16.4 seconds.

No prices have been announced, but it is likely to cost around £2000 in Germany."

The Type 901

The Type 901 started life as the Type 695. Work began on this project in late 1959, with the body receiving the T-7 designation; interesting, considering that the first 356B had a T-5 shell, while the later 356B and 356C each had a T-6 type. The front of the T-7 proposal would be carried over to the Type 901, but the roofline, glasshouse and rear-end were all modified over the next few years.

The wheelbase was a key factor in all this. A longer wheelbase had been chosen to provide better accommodation in the rear, but internal wrangling and a last minute decision to stick to a proven formula of providing 2+2 seating (rather than a full four-seater) resulted in a wheelbase slightly longer than that of the 356, but an awful lot shorter than that specified for the 695 styling proposal (which duly became the Type 754 running prototype in 1960). Ultimately, it was listed at 2211mm (87.0in.) in the catalogue, and the roofline was adjusted to suit the new arrangement, forming a gentle curve that ran down from the top of the windscreen to the tail.

Compared to the 356, the 911 was slightly longer (mainly due to the longer wheelbase employed on the six-

cylinder car) and lower, but narrower, despite the track dimensions being far greater. The now classic lines of the 911 were penned by Butzi Porsche (officially Ferdinand Alexander Porsche – Ferry's oldest son), while Erwin Komenda did the engineering side of the bodywork in conjunction with Reutter, the latter ultimately being bought by Porsche before production of the new car began.

The powerplant was also all-new, although its roots could be traced back to the eight-cylinder Grand Prix engine. The flat-eight F1 unit was first run in December 1960, and gave Porsche its first – and only – Grand Prix win at the 1962 French GP. It also formed the basis for the Type 771 unit used in the contemporary sports-racers fielded by the factory.

A number of designs were tried before the flat-six was given the green light for series production. The definitive engine, which, like the rest of the new car, also carried the Type 901 designation, first appeared in the autumn of 1963. Overseen by Hans Tomala, it was a two-litre, air-cooled unit with a chain-driven single overhead camshaft per bank. To overcome oil surge during hard cornering, it had dry sump lubrication.

With a bore and stroke of 80 x 66mm, cubic capacity was 1991cc; this produced 130bhp at 6100rpm, giving a specific output of 65bhp per litre. All early production engines had aluminium alloy castings and a two-part crankcase. The cylinders used Biral construction (cast-iron barrels surrounded by finned aluminium castings for cooling), and the cylinder heads were of light alloy. Originally, three single-choke downdraught Solex carburettors were used on each bank, but these were later replaced, from the beginning of 1966, by triple-choke Webers.

The five-speed gearbox-cum-transaxle was developed jointly for the 901 and the 904 racer (more on which later). It featured a dog-leg first, down and to the left against a spring, with second through fifth being in a traditional 'H' pattern to the right of it. The gearing was very long-legged, with overdriven fourth and top.

In its final form, the front suspension consisted of a lower A-arm and MacPherson strut combined with a 19mm (0.75in) diameter longitudinal torsion bar on each side; a 13mm (0.51in) anti-roll bar was fitted up front. This new arrangement not only improved control but also freed up valuable luggage space.

At the back, a trailing arm ran off a transverse torsion bar (23mm in diameter, or 0.90in) towards the wheel, while another tubular link, with a pivot point near the nose of the gearbox, located the hub and formed what amounted to a trailing wishbone. The telescopic shock absorber (sourced from Koni, as were the front dampers, and incorporating progressively acting rubber buffers for enhanced control) was fitted as far away from the torsion bar as possible in order to give it the maximum amount of travel.

The rack-and-pinion steering came from ZF, and was unusual in that it featured central attachment of the steering column to enable Porsche to produce lhd and rhd cars with equal ease. The braking system was much the same as that employed on the 356, with discs up front and the novel disc/drum arrangement at the rear. Surprisingly, the skinny wheels and tyres were also carried over from the earlier model.

Inside, the feeling of light and space was the biggest difference compared with the 356. Otherwise, there was a lot that would have been familiar to a Porsche fan, especially the seats. Incidentally, the two gauges seen on the dashboard of the 901 prototypes were replaced by five dials on production models; this became something of a 911 signature.

Porsche changed the 901 name to 911 following a complaint from Peugeot regarding the use of "their" numbering system (although Bristol had similar model designations and the Porsche racers were left unchallenged) before it went on sale to the public in September 1964. Introduced at DM 21,900, it was a touch cheaper than the 356-based Carrera 2, but with such a relatively high price, it was obviously aimed at connoisseurs rather than fleet buyers.

One era ends, another begins

Although America had begun receiving 911s a few months earlier, the first right-hand drive cars were delivered to the UK in May 1965. Shortly after, there was a change in the gearing, with slightly lower ratios than before; the same gearbox (Type 902/1) was also employed for the 912 series.

The 912 was introduced in May 1965. The body, suspension, steering and braking system was identical to that of the six-cylinder 911, but the 912, launched at DM 16,250, was far closer to the 356 in that it used a slightly modified version of the four-cylinder Super 90 power unit (known as the 616/16 in its ultimate 95bhp form).

While the 356 soldiered on in America for a few more months, the 912 replaced it in Europe with immediate effect. Powered by the 616/36 unit, which boasted a 1582cc cubic capacity and developed 90bhp DIN, the 912 came with either a four- or five-speed manual transmission.

The 912 proved very popular and, in order to keep up with demand and reduce pressure on the overstretched Reutter works, some bodies were built at Karmann.

Racing news

Ferry Porsche gave the go-ahead for the new mid-engined 904 competition car at the end of 1962. The lightweight glassfibre body (this material was chosen to speed up production, as four or five cars had to be built each day if the new model was to be homologated for the 1964 season) was bonded to the chassis for extra strength. Records show that 120 were built: 104 were made and sold with the four-cylinder Carrera engines and, of the 16 904s retained by the factory, ten had six-cylinder engines and six had the eight-cylinder unit.

The new model's first major race was at Sebring in March 1964, where it ran as a prototype: it was eventually homologated in April. Shortly after, the 904 driven by Colin Davis and Antonio Pucci won the 1964 Targa Florio, with Linge and Balzarini finishing second. Ultimately, the 904 dominated two-litre sports car racing during the 1964 and 1965 seasons.

Ferry Porsche had already approved production of another 100

Early advertising for the four-cylinder 912.

904s for the 1966 season, but then Ferdinand Piech took over the Research & Development Department and, therefore, the competition shop. Piech (the son of Ferry's sister, he'd joined the company in 1963) had grander ideas and from now on Porsche's philosophy on racing changed, with the cars moving further and further away from their road-going counterparts. Piech set the marque down the road of producing pure racers, culminating in the all-conquering 917.

Among numerous outstanding victories, Porsche won the Targa Florio in 1966, 1967, 1968, 1969 and 1970 (all with different drivers), and again in 1973. However, in September 1971, Ernst Fuhrmann returned to the Porsche camp following a tenure at the Goetze piston ring company and duly took Piech's place as head of engineering. It's interesting to note, given the close bond between race and road machines in the 356 era, that Fuhrmann considered

The beautiful 904 racer (right) with a contemporary 911.

A 1967 model year 911S Targa.

the current breed of racers too far removed from the road vehicles to be of any real use in marketing. It will be remembered that not long after his new appointment, a whole range of sporting machinery stemmed from the 911 and, once again, Porsche road and racing cars were unequivocally linked.

The Targa model

The 1965 Frankfurt Show saw the debut of the Targa model, although, like the coupé it was based on, it was some time before production models filtered through to the dealerships. (Indeed, it wasn't until the end of 1966 that the first Targas left the lines at Zuffenhausen.)

Nonetheless, the press was excited at the prospect of this new variation, which brought back open Porsche motoring after the departure of the 356 Cabriolet. *Auto Topics* noted in its January 1966 edition: "The new Porsche features a roll bar, and offers a new way of top down-top up driving in comfort. Roll bars so far have been used only in Grand Prix cars and prototypes, but Porsche now becomes the first automobile manufacturer to make it a production feature.

"A detachable roof in matching finish converts the car into a hardtop,

19

and with easy to operate snap fasteners attached to the roll bar and windshield the conversion is completed without effort. The soft-top version is equally easy to operate, stretching from roll bar to windshield. With the rear window closed and the top down, you have your own sunroof."

An open car had always been an essential part of the Porsche line-up, so it was not surprising that a 911-based version was built. The Targa was, however, something of a compromise. Butzi Porsche had wanted all-new panels for the rear but, due to cost limitations, the old metalwork had to be incorporated into the design. With the need to keep rigidity in the bodyshell (always a problem with closed cars converted into open ones), the Targa roll-over bar was put forward and duly developed.

As announced at the Frankfurt Show, there was a reinforced plastic panel for the roof section, augmented by a fabric cover that could be used when the former was not in place. However, no amount of experimental work could stop the fabric from ballooning at speed, and this idea was eventually shelved. What resulted was a single folding roof panel that fitted neatly in the luggage compartment when not in use.

Early press pictures had padding on the box-section stainless steel roll bar, but for production models this was changed to a natural brushed finish. One thing which was carried over from the show car was the removable rear window. Produced in heavyweight clear plastic, it could be unzipped when wished.

By an amazing stroke of luck,

the Targa was put forward before the Federal proposal that effectively outlawed open sports cars in the States. While the Targa would have met the safety requirements outlined, many manufacturers – and particularly those in England – were thrown into a state of panic by this bombshell. Ultimately, the ruling was never passed. Its announcement, however, was to influence car design for the best part of a decade.

The Targa body was available for both the 911 and 912, incidentally. As it happens, the 100,000th Porsche was actually a 912 Targa, ordered by the Baden-Württemberg police force, and built on 21 December 1966. Early Targa production was restricted to left-hand drive – a situation that did not change until the 2.4-litre cars arrived in the early 1970s.

"Reliability on the race track, safety on the street."

The 911S

Announced in August 1966, the 911S was given a 160bhp version of the flat-six and a unique five-speed gearbox with a taller top ratio to endow the car with 140mph (225kph) performance. The S stood for Super, and this was probably a fair description of the vehicle.

In line with the hike in performance, the suspension and braking system was uprated, with adjustable Koni shocks, a rear anti-roll bar to go with the beefier one at the front, and ventilated discs. Fuchs forged aluminium alloys also came as part of the package.

The trim was slightly different on the S – both inside and out – although all cars were subject to numerous changes for the 1967 season. The most obvious changes included new badging, revised dashboard trim, the adoption of an Ebonite steering wheel (leather covered on the S), and gauge revisions. On the mechanical front, the driveshaft design was changed to incorporate Rzeppa joints, the 130bhp engine was given milder cams, and the heat exchangers were modified to improve exhaust flow and longevity.

The 911S brought back the three-tier Porsche line-up of the past, with the 912 providing an entry level model, the strict 911 in the middle, and the 911S covering the sector once covered by the Carrera. And, of course, the Targa gave the buyer the alternative of open car motoring.

Progress of the 911 series

The 1968 model year saw the introduction of the A-Serie 911s (earlier cars were known by the O-Serie designation). For Europe, the 911T (T standing for Touring) was introduced, with 110bhp coming from its less exotic two-litre six. At the same time, the standard 911 became the 911L (Luxus), whilst the 911S and 912 continued unchanged.

The 911T was quite basic compared to the other six-cylinder models, but it inherited the wider wheel rims and dual-circuit brakes introduced that year. It was also available with the new Sportomatic transmission option, a semi-automatic version of the four-speed gearbox, which received some fairly mixed reaction from the motoring press.

Numerous detail changes were applied to the range, many introduced in order to satisfy Federal regulations. Amongst other things, instrument bezels became black (while calibrations changed from green on black to white on black), there were new mirrors inside and out, new door handles, and revised trim on the doors and dashboard. In addition, the S got new sill covers, and a fixed glass rear window became optional on the Targa.

The Americans had a different line-up for 1968. There was no S, and no 911T. Instead, two 130bhp models were listed (the 911 and 911L) alongside the 912, using air injection (AI) to overcome emissions laws, and featuring revised headlights (distinguished by the wide chrome rim) and side markers on the body (although the latter was for 1968 only, as the reflectors were incorporated in the combination lights for the following season).

Meanwhile, the 911 proved itself to be an excellent rally car, with Gunther Klass winning the 1966 European Rally Championship; Porsche drivers Vic Elford and Sobieslav Zasada duly won the two ERC titles available in 1967, with 'Quick Vic' driving a 911R on occasion. The 911R was a lightweight machine modified by Karl Bauer. Featuring a 210bhp engine bored out to give 2247cc, this was the direct link that gave rise to the RS/RSR series of later years. Only 22 were built, but the 911R has a very special place in history.

1968 saw Porsche win in Sweden, Monte Carlo, San Remo, East Germany and West Germany, with Pauli Toivonen lifting the ERC trophy at the end of the year. By this time, the 911R had been tried with a new 916 racing engine, and Porsche had entered the London-Sydney Marathon with a reasonable degree of success.

On the racing front, as well as the long-distance races, the 911 series excelled at the shorter SCCA meetings in the States. By the end of the decade, the 911 had picked up Class victories in almost every major event in Europe and America. What was even more impressive was the way the model was able to challenge for overall honours on a number of occasions.

The B-Serie models

Development of the 911 continued at quite a pace, with the 1969 models being of particular importance. Not surprisingly, given Porsche's policy of constant evolution, a new generation 911/912 (the B-Serie) was launched in September 1968, with a 57mm (2.2in) longer wheelbase and flared wheelarches covering wider wheels and tyres.

Fuel-injection was added to the 911E (the replacement for the 911L, with E standing for einspritz, German for injection) and 911S, giving cleaner emissions yet allowing 10bhp more to be extracted from each unit at the same time. This enabled both engines to qualify for the American market, and both grades went on sale alongside the 911T and 912 for 1969; in other words, the line-up was once again the same all over the world.

In addition to the fuel-injected engines, the other big news for 1969 was the longer wheelbase. This was achieved by lengthening the trailing arms at the rear; the engine and gearbox didn't move. As such, the wheels were simply shifted rearward, driven by different halfshafts with bigger Rzeppa joints to allow for the extra stress involved with the shafts being angled backward, and the suspension and bodywork modified to suit. Thus, the overall length of the car remained the same.

Other features for this season – the last in which the 912 was sold – included a new ZF steering rack and steering wheel, larger brake pads, adoption of hydropneumatic self-levelling struts for the front of the 911E (optional on other cars), magnesium alloy crankcases (transmission casings were also produced in this lightweight material later on), capacitive discharge (CD) ignition for the injected models, twin batteries on six-cylinder cars to replace the single item used previously, improved gearboxes with revised ratios, a new heating and ventilation system, and modified trim inside and out – again!

New combination lamps were used, with new horn grilles up front and reflectors added at the rear. The Targa also received a revised roll-over bar design and the fixed rear window was declared standard (along

A 911T Targa for the 1969 season, when the long wheelbase cars made their debut.

with tinted glass); front quarterlights retained their opening facility on the Targa, even though they became fixed on the coupé from this point.

Porsche won in Monte Carlo again in 1969, with ERC victories following in Sweden, Greece and Corsica; Gerard Larrousse and Maurice Gelin provided a highlight on the racing calendar by winning the Tour de France Automobile in an ultra lightweight 911R.

With production now up to 70 cars a day (the figure would increase again soon, largely thanks to a great deal of expansion at Zuffenhausen), a total of 15,292 Porsches were built in 1969, but fewer than 6000 made the journey across the Atlantic to America. Compared with recent US sales performance, especially if taken as a percentage of production, this has to be considered rather disappointing.

A joint project with VW

The history of Porsche and Volkswagen had been entwined since the foundation of both great concerns, and it's fair to say that, without one, the other would not have existed, as Professor Porsche designed the VW Beetle, the car that provided the basis for Ferry Porsche's roadster after the war.

After signing an agreement in 1948, as well as allowing Porsche access to components and use of the Volkswagen sales and service network, VW's Heinz Nordhoff had provided the Stuttgart firm with a constant stream of commissions.

In view of the vast history shared by Porsche and Volkswagen, it was perhaps inevitable that the two companies should at some stage produce a joint project. That time came in the mid-1960s when both concerns were faced with a dilemma:

the Stuttgart firm needed a new entry level machine, and VW needed a replacement for the Karmann Ghia.

Eventually it was agreed that a new sports car would be developed by Porsche, with two versions being built: a VW four-cylinder model and a Porsche variant powered by the familiar flat-six. Both concerns were happy, as Volkswagen got Porsche's expertise in an area in which it had little experience, and Porsche got bodies cheaply, as VW would pay for the tooling and development costs. The result was the 914 series.

Ferry Porsche and Heinz Nordhoff had enjoyed a splendid working relationship for many years, but Nordhoff was due to retire in 1970. In preparation, Kurt Lotz was brought in as Nordhoff's deputy to gradually take over the reins in mid-1967. However, Nordhoff became seriously ill shortly

An early four-cylinder 914. The six-cylinder version was dropped from the line-up not long after the mid-engined line was introduced.

after, giving the newcomer no time at all to learn of Nordhoff's arrangements regarding the 914.

On the 1 March 1968, the first prototype 914 was driven, but then, a few weeks later, Professor Nordhoff died. Lotz knew nothing of the 'gentleman's agreement' for the supply of 914 bodies from Karmann. Although this wasn't unusual, as the two men often worked on a verbal deal, quite naturally, Lotz wanted to see something in writing. Eventually, after much negotiation, an agreement was reached whereby Porsche and Volkswagen would form a separate company, both partners having a 50 per cent holding.

The plan was announced in January 1969, and the following April, VW-Porsche Vertriebsgesellschaft GmbH (or VG

for short) was established in Stuttgart with a working capital of DM 5 million. This new concern would be responsible for the marketing and distribution of the VW-Porsche 914 series and the 911 in most markets, with the notable exception of America, which would have its own sales organization.

Although on the face of it this seemed a rather dramatic move, it was, in effect, little more than making a previous arrangement official, as Porsche cars were distributed through VW outlets everywhere except Britain and France. Nonetheless, the announcement sent rumours around the globe about a possible merger until they were quashed by a blunt Stuttgart press release.

Approximately 30,000 912 Porsches were produced from 1965 to 1969, before its place in the line-up

was taken by the 914. As mentioned earlier, there were to be two different models. The Volkswagen version, the 914/4, would be powered by the 1679cc, air-cooled, flat-four engine from the 411E model using VW's new electronic injection system, allowing it to meet all American emission requirements (including those for California). The Porsche model, known as the 914/6, would be equipped with the classic six-cylinder air-cooled engine from the 1969 model year 911T, chosen for the 914/6 as this kept the new model at two litres.

Part of the agreement with Volkswagen stipulated that the 914 range would be badged as a VW-Porsche. The only exception to this rule was in America, where all models would be called Porsches, regardless of the powerplant.

23

of 1970. Like so many of the Stuttgart thoroughbreds, it went to a buyer in the States.

Porsche in competition

Porsche had a reputation to uphold. The company won the Manufacturers' Championship in 1969, and, in May of that year, built 25 examples of the Type 917. The model's first victory came in a minor race at Zeltweg towards the end of 1969. A revised version called the 917K arrived in time for the 1970 Daytona 24-hour race.

At Le Mans that year, the Porsche marque dominated the legendary 24-hour race to take the first of many overall victories at the Sarthe circuit. Porsche veteran, Hans Herrmann, and Britain's Richard Attwood took their Austrian-entered 917K to victory, followed home by two other Porsches. There was no looking back, as the 917 totally dominated the racing scene for the next four years.

As far as the 911 was concerned, it continued its versatile career in racing and rallying, winning the Monte Carlo Rally for the third time in a row in 1970, thanks to Bjorn Waldegaard. Waldegaard won again in Sweden and Austria, with Porsche taking the ERC title at the end of the year.

Sobieslav Zasada was declared European Rally Champion again in 1971, but the 911's heyday was over. On the race tracks, too, it was clear that the whole racing circus had become a more professional affair, and the days of challenging the top runners in a virtually standard 911 were numbered.

Porsche failed to contest the 1972 World Championship as the new regulations, which introduced a three-litre engine capacity limit, didn't suit the German firm. Instead, it turned its attention to the Can-Am series, the works cars proudly displaying the Porsche and Audi names side-by-side

The 2.2-litre cars

The major changes applied to the 1969 model year 911s were carried over to the C-Serie cars of 1970, although the 912 was dropped and the six-cylinder engine was bored out to give 2195cc. Introduced in September 1969, the 2.2-litre machines came with power outputs now quoted at 125bhp, 155bhp, and 180bhp DIN respectively for the T, E and S grades.

A number of engine and drivetrain changes accompanied the bigger bore dimension (up from 80mm to 84mm), giving the latest Porsches greater flexibility and a far more refined level of performance. In addition, to cope with the extra power, ventilated discs were fitted across the board, although the 911T had cast-iron calipers rather than the light alloy ones fitted to the 911E and 911S.

Cars were now sold in the States through the newly-formed Porsche+Audi sales organization, with Volkswagens distributed through separate showrooms for the 1970 season. However, the stronger economy in Germany led in turn to a weaker dollar, making cars like Porsches very expensive.

The value of the deutschmark had risen steadily against the dollar after the 914 was launched (by early 1972, the deutschmark stood at DM 3.2 to the dollar – it had been DM 4.0 in late 1969). Not only did this make imported cars more expensive, but if a price was retained in America, it also gave less return for the manufacturer in dollar sales.

In fact, by the close of 1970 VW-Porsche's financial results were so bad that they seriously considered abandoning the entire 914 project. After all, a loss of DM 200 million is not something to be taken lightly. Despite reservations, the decision was taken to continue developing the 914, and a number of detail improvements were duly made.

Compared to earlier years, there were very few changes for the 1971 model year 911 series. The 150,000th Porsche was a 911S coupé, incidentally, built during the summer on the coachwork. It won the series easily in 1972, and then repeated this success the following year.

The 2.4-litre range

The 2.4-litre range was introduced at the 1971 Frankfurt Show. The bore size was carried over, but the stroke was increased, thus giving a larger displacement of 2341cc. More power was the result, although just as importantly, emissions were cut and fuel consumption enhanced. There were three engine options, giving 130bhp, 165bhp, and 190bhp DIN in European guise (the entry level US power unit had 140bhp, thanks to the adoption of fuel-injection).

A new five-speed gearbox, with a more conventional shift pattern featuring fifth outside the traditional 'H', was also adopted, signalling the end of the dog-leg first layout. The four-speed unit was based on this new transmission, and the four-speed Sportomatic continued to be offered as an alternative.

The quickest way to recognize a 1972 model is via the oil tank filler on the offside rear wing following relocation of the tank itself, although this arrangement lasted only one season. A front spoiler was adopted on the 911S (initially an option on the T and E grades), and black trim became more prominent. Apart from a few other minor detail differences, it was pretty difficult to distinguish a 1972 coupé from a 1971 vehicle.

Corporate matters

A new five-man steering committee

Gerard Larrousse on the 1972 Monte Carlo Rally.

had been established in April 1971, with members that included Ferry and Butzi Porsche, Ferdinand and Michael Piech, and Heinz Branitzki (the gentleman who looked after the firm's finances following the retirement of Hans Kern).

In the background, though, trouble was brewing. Ferry Porsche realised that the sheer number of Porsche and Piech family members involved in top positions within the company was definitely going to cause severe problems if the rivalry that was starting to set in escalated. Corporate moves were announced that effectively allowed everyone to withdraw with honour, and signalled the return of Ernst Fuhrmann to Porsche late in 1971. This was only the beginning.

On 1 March 1972 the Porsche company was reorganized. Three concerns – Dr Ing. h. c. F. Porsche KG in Zuffenhausen, the VW-Porsche VG in Ludwigsburg, and the Porsche Konstruktion KG in Salzburg – came under the control of a holding company, Porsche GmbH, registered in Stuttgart. Ferry Porsche and Louise Piech were Managing Directors, with Ernst Fuhrmann responsible for engineering, and Heinz Branitzki appointed Finance Director. The Development Manager was Helmuth Bott (who reported directly to Fuhrmann), the Sales Director was L. Schmidt, H. Kurtz was named head of production, and K. Kalkbrenner was in charge of the Personnel Department.

As far as the car business in Zuffenhausen was concerned (Porsche per se in the eyes of the public), all of the members of the Porsche family withdrew officially, with Fuhrmann (named as Chairman) and Branitzki in charge. The reorganization was completed when Porsche became a joint stock company: Dr Ing. h. c. F. Porsche AG.

After the family split, Butzi Porsche formed Porsche Design (a highly successful consultancy), and Ferdinand Piech went to VW-Audi, helping to develop Audi's 4wd system which led to the world-beating Audi Quattro. Before too long he was the head of the German firm. Both men left a legacy at Porsche; no-one will ever forget the racing cars, especially the 917, nurtured by Piech, whilst Ferdinand Porsche III gave us the classic lines of the 911.

A total of 14,265 911s were built in the 1972 calendar year (as opposed to the 1972 MY), a significant increase on 1971, when the company was hit by a poor home economy and a series of strikes. Of this total, six out of every ten built were coupés, with 60 per cent being Ts, 16 per cent Es, and 22 per cent Ss.

In the meantime, important events were taking place at Volkswagen. VW had once again lost money in 1971, and the following year Opel overtook it as the leading German manufacturer in terms of output. Lotz resigned in September 1971, with Rudolf Leiding taking his place. Leiding was a production specialist, and it was obvious that he supported the new direction brought about by the K70.

Originally an Audi-NSU prototype, it catapulted VW into the world of fwd water-cooled machines. Introduced as the VW K70 in 1971, it spelt the end of the NSU marque, casting doubt on the potential future of an air-cooled, mid-engined vehicle.

914 developments

Initial sales of the 914/6 had looked promising, but demand quickly tailed off. In the first year, 2657 were built – well under the expected 6000 sales worldwide. During the second year, it was obvious that the six-cylinder machine wasn't going to sell, and production was cut back dramatically for the 1972 model year. In fact, only 229 cars were constructed.

Plans to introduce a bigger-engined six-cylinder model at the 1971 Paris Salon were duly shelved, the stillborn 916 remaining nothing more than a series of promising prototypes. The 914/6 didn't appear in the 1973 model year line-up, and total production for the type amounted to just 3318 units.

With no 914/6, a new 100bhp, two-litre, four-cylinder model was introduced to take its place; to meet ever stricter emissions regulations in the USA there was a new 1.7-litre unit for the American market.

Thanks to the new two-litre 914 and general improvements made to the range, the 1973 model year was to be the 914's most successful sales period, with annual production ending just 10 per cent short of the original target of 30,000 units a year. With most of the production going to America, this was no mean feat, as the exchange rate was now less than DM 2.5 to the dollar.

The Volkswagen Type 412 had been introduced for the 1973 model year. The 412 power unit went to 1795cc for 1974 in the heavier four-door and estate models, and was also used in the Transporter light commercial series. For 1974, the same engine replaced the 1.7-litre lump for the 914 series as well.

When the new generation of 911s with impact bumpers was launched in September 1973, it was noted that engine sizes had been increased again, this time to 2.7-litres for the mainstream cars, with three-litre powerplants for the top models. This

The star of the 1973 model year was the 2.7-litre Carrera RS, seen here with the early style 'Carrera' decal (production models had negative script, not positive as it was in the original catalogue). Behind the Carrera is a 911E coupé.

took them even further away from the 914 series in terms of performance and refinement.

A number of 914 limited editions and specials were announced, but sales still fell. In America, the subject of pricing again raised its ugly head. In the July 1974 edition of *Road Test* magazine, it was noted: "The 914 was branded 'overpriced' when it was $2000-$3000 cheaper than it is now, which supposedly elevates it into the outrageously overpriced category and the 911, which costs about twice as much, into the scandalously overpriced bracket." There was nothing that could be done – after all, the exchange rates dictated the price, and the Porsche range was barely in line with them.

A 911 update

While the standard 1973 model year 911 range was much the same as it had been in the 1972 season, there was an important introduction at the 1972 Paris Salon – the 2.7-litre Carrera RS. With a capacity of 2687cc (90 x 70.4mm), the 210bhp Carrera RS was a stripped out road racer

with a lightened body featuring a rear spoiler, flared arches covering a wider wheel and tyre combination, and an uprated suspension.

The RS came in three different specifications: the DM 33,000 Sport version (M471); the more civilized M472 Touring variant (with 911S style trim), or racing guise (the 2.8-litre M491, better known as the legendary RSR).

In reality, this was Fuhrmann's vision of the future Porsche racing programme. To qualify the car for Group 4, a minimum of 500 units had to be sold, and while the RSR was the weapon of choice for top level competition, the RS would make up the numbers, providing the owner with either a fast road car, or a less potent racing machine.

The RS/RSR series quickly established itself as the car to beat in all corners of the world, with Peter Gregg winning the SCCA Trans-Am and IMSA GT titles, and Porsche taking 23 of the 27 podium places available in the 1973 European GT Championship.

The International Race of Champions (or IROC) provided an

interesting branch of 911 racing history, as the three-litre, normally-aspirated IROC racers were basically the first of a new breed of RS/RSR models, 15 of them delivered late in 1973 for the American series.

Meanwhile, new Federal requirements changed the look of the 911 forever. Proposed 1974 bumper regulations were actually postponed until the following season for sports cars. However, while the 914 took advantage of the reprieve, the 911 was ready, and a new generation was launched at the 1973 Frankfurt Show.

The traditional T, E, and S designations were dropped in favour of a basic 911 grade, a new 911S, and a Carrera topping the line-up. These all had 2.7-litre engines, the Carrera unit being carried over from the 1973 RS, and the other two coming with Bosch K-Jetronic fuel-injection.

The Carrera had the same bulging wings as its predecessor, but all cars gained new safety bumpers to comply with the US regulations. It was actually a very neat piece of design work, bringing the vehicle up-

The 1974 model year brought with it a new generation of 2.7-litre cars with so-called 'safety bumpers' – introduced in response to Federal requirements due to take effect the following season. This is the strict 911 Targa (as opposed to the 911S version).

911

to-date without losing too much of the character. With the bumpers now in body colour, more black trim was added, and a number of changes were applied to the interior, including new high-back seats, new steering wheels, and a new fascia panel with revised switches and vents at either end.

Stark reality

In 1974, Volkswagen had been forced to cut back the workforce, despite the launch of the new Passat/Dasher. Other new generation water-cooled cars like the Golf/Rabbit (and the Audi range) eventually pulled the company out of trouble, but for a moment, there was a serious danger that the business would fail and have to close its doors permanently.

By July 1974, when Karmann Ghia production finally ceased, over 360,000 coupés and more than 80,000 cabriolets had been built. It

was replaced by an altogether more modern vehicle – the Giugiaro-styled Scirocco.

As Ferry Porsche stated in his book, *Cars Are My Life*: "This complete change of policy by VW naturally called into question the existence of the joint distribution company, the break-up of which had already been recommended by members of the VW supervisory board. Finally, on 8 May 1974, an agreement to that effect was signed. We acquired VW's stake and moved our sales department into the VG building in Ludwigsburg."

The agreement was retroactive to 1 January 1974, and ended a very uneasy partnership in which both parties seemed to be pulling in opposite directions. Full control of the 914 shifted to Porsche, although a clause in the agreement ensured that from the outside, it would seem as though nothing had changed. Interestingly,

a number of development contracts were cancelled, although Volkswagen and Porsche did not entirely forsake their long-running alliance.

911 sales were slow for Porsche in the first part of 1974, but, fortunately, picked up as the season progressed. There was a new three-litre RS/RSR series for 1974 (based on the IROC racers, and built as an 'evolution' of the earlier models). With the standard range priced at between DM 29,250 and DM 41,950, the new 2993cc RS was extremely expensive, commanding the best part of DM 65,000.

The new RS/RSR was basically a customer racer (Group 3 or Group 4), while the works entered Group 5 with a 2142cc turbocharged model; with the FIA multiplying the displacement by 1.4 due to forced induction, it took the car right up to the three-litre limit. The latest cars dominated the European GT Championship and the IMSA series, and the Martini sponsored Group 5 monsters provided the basis for Porsche's assault on the World Championship of Makes, due for inauguration in 1975 but ultimately delayed until the following year.

A turbocharged future

In 1975 revised gearing was introduced to reduce engine revs, plus a new three-speed Sportomatic transmission for the majority of models (it was adopted across the board for 1976). But the big news was the Turbo. As Ferry Porsche explained: "The exhaust gas turbocharger is capable not only of achieving considerable increases in performance, but also of improving the efficiency of the engine and thus saving fuel. The technology involved was nothing new to us when we came to use it in competition cars, since we had already used it during the war in our air-cooled diesel engines for tanks. Having been subjected to rigorous tests in our competition cars, the turbocharger then found its way into our production cars."

A prototype Turbo had been shown at Frankfurt in 1973, but the 1974 Paris Salon saw the debut of the real thing. Not only was this the quickest road car to come from the Stuttgart factory during this period, it was also the most expensive – at DM 65,800, the 2993cc machine was literally twice the price of a 911 coupé (then listed at DM 32,350 in March 1975). However, despite a hefty price tag and the relentless rise in fuel costs, within 18 months of its launch, Porsche had already sold twice the number originally expected.

With bulging wheelarches, a massive whaletail spoiler, luxury trim, and stunning performance, the 260bhp Porsche Turbo stole sales from the Italian exotics, with deliveries beginning in earnest after the 1975 Geneva Show.

End of the 914

Changes to the 914 for 1975 were headed by a different bumper design to meet the latest US regulations, and a modified two-litre engine for the States to satisfy even stricter emissions laws, including a catalytic converter and extra anti-pollution equipment for California, thus making the cars costlier to produce.

In Germany, the price was held on standard models, but in America, the exchange rate and additional costs involved in meeting the emissions regulations pushed even the basic 914-1.8 to $6300. Add options to this, and it became a very expensive car.

The two-litre 914 was priced at $7250 against $10,845 for the 912E – a fuel-injected revamp on the old 912 theme to keep the American dealers happy until the 924 arrived on US shores. While the latter could hardly be classed as cheap, it should be borne in mind that the 911S coupé was $13,845 at the time, and the Targa-bodied version no less than $14,795.

On 10 February 1975, Toni Schmucker, an ex-Ford man, took over from Rudolf Leiding at Volkswagen. Carrying on from where Leiding left off, the 1795cc VW engine was stopped for the 1976 MY in the VW range when the Transporter series (the only model

The Carrera RS 3.0 was really a competition model, although it also made an excellent road car.

A press photograph released to illustrate the 1976 model year, although careful inspection of the cars reveals a number of features left over from the previous season, such as the old-style rear spoiler on the Turbo.

other than the 914 to still use it) went to two-litres, using basically the same engine as found in the larger of the two 914s. For this reason, only the 914-2.0 was offered for 1976.

Markets were either shrinking, disappearing, or becoming increasingly difficult to satisfy legally. Because of this, the decision was taken to run down production to an absolute minimum and sell the 914 series only in America for 1976 – it was about the only country where any sort of demand existed, at least at a level where a profit could be made.

The last cars were completed in Karmann's Osnabruck works during the early part of 1976, with final sales taking place in the spring. No announcement was made; the 914 was simply allowed to fade away.

Although the 914 wasn't quite the sales success Porsche had hoped for, almost 120,000 were built over the model's six year production run.

The 924

The 924 project was originally a design commissioned by Volkswagen under the number EA-425. Almost from the moment the 914 was launched, Volkswagen had been considering the details for its more conventional successor, and the Type 924 was it.

However, at the last minute, just as the model had reached the pre-production stage, the management at Volkswagen cancelled it. Due to a combination of political wrangling and the energy crisis, the consensus at VW was that it would be too expensive to produce. Porsche was given the opportunity to buy back the

design to put into production itself, which it did.

The 924 was exactly what Porsche needed in the hard economic times of the 1970s. Sales had fallen off considerably, and just 9424 cars were produced in Stuttgart in 1975. However, sales would soon pick up with the introduction of the low-priced 924 in November 1975. At last, Porsche had the entry level machine it had originally been trying for with the 914.

The 924 was a great departure from traditional Porsche practice. The engine was a water-cooled, 1984cc, four-cylinder unit mounted at the front, with rear-wheel drive through a transaxle system (i.e. a gearbox combined with the rear axle). With an overhead camshaft and K-Jetronic fuel-injection, the two-litre unit developed a modest 125bhp, but powered the car to 125mph (200kph) and gave excellent fuel economy.

The elegant body was designed by the Dutchman, Harm Lagaay, under the supervision of Tony Lapine. It was a wedge-shaped 2+2 coupé with smooth lines and a large glass hatch at the rear – even today, it looks surprisingly modern, thanks to some fine detailing.

Naturally enough, considering that the 924 was going to be part of the VW-Audi range, the vehicle used a large number of parts sourced from that organisation (including the engine block, suspension components, and many interior fittings), and was actually assembled at the old NSU factory.

The 924 made it into America as an early 1977 model year car, superceding the 912E in the spring of 1976. At just $9395, it was some $4600 cheaper than a 911S coupé, and more than $1000 cheaper than the short-lived model it replaced. The car was an instant hit, making up more than 13,500 of the 20,000 Porsche sales made in the States that year.

The 911 line matures

With the 2.7-litre cars undergoing a few detail changes only, and the Turbo, as a new car, being treated much the same, it was the Carrera that received the most attention for 1976. Not available in the States, the Carrera was basically a normally-aspirated version of the Turbo, and with 200bhp on tap, it was an interesting alternative, over DM 20,000 cheaper than the Porsche supercar.

Refinement was the order of the day, with more emphasis placed on comfort rather than outright performance, and all the time there was growing concern about the environment to keep in mind. Porsche was already looking at stratified-charge and lean-burn engines, but it also supported a full racing

The Carrera 3.0 seen here was not sold in the States, although it provided the basis for a new generation of 911s introduced for the 1978 season.

An American poster announcing a Porsche victory at Daytona in 1977.

programme in order to develop new technologies.

For 1976, Porsche had the 934 (the Turbo RSR), the 935, and the 936. Ultimately, Porsche won the World Championship for Sports Cars (using Group 6 models), and the World Championship for Makes (for Group 5 Silhouette Sports Cars) in 1976. More effort was directed toward the Group 5 series in 1977, enabling the Stuttgart marque to easily retain its title. The 935 was a memorable machine in a memorable era.

A few detail changes were applied to the 911 range for 1977, with 16-inch wheels for the Turbo, minor engine and gearbox modifications for the 2.7-litre cars, and a few interior revisions on all models.

A new Porsche was announced at this time: introduced in February 1977, the 928 made its public debut at the following month's Geneva Show. It was a member of the same family as the 924, with a front-mounted, water-cooled engine and transaxle to give good weight distribution. The engine, in this instance, however, was a V8 unit of 4.5 litres designed to tempt customers who traditionally bought from the likes of Jaguar and Mercedes-Benz. The brainchild of Dr Fuhrmann, it was immediately voted 'Car of the Year.'

In actual fact, work on the 928 had started before the 924 project, as at one point it was put forward as the possible successor to the 911 range. However, when the Type 924 passed to Porsche ownership, because the need for a cheaper car was greater, it was the smaller-engined model that went into production first.

Shortly after the 928 made its debut, the cost of 911 motoring increased yet again, with roughly DM 1400 added to the range. The Turbo now stood at DM 70,000 – some DM 15,000 more than the 928 at the time of its announcement.

A total of 19,896 Porsches were sold in the States during 1977, but only 6226 of these were 911s (517 Turbos); the rest were 924s, as the 928 did not appear in America until the 1978 season. By this time, a new 911 series had made its debut.

The 1978 model year
For 1978, the NA 911 series became known as the 911SC (the SC standing for Super Carrera). This was a similar machine to the European Carrera offered in 1976 and 1977, powered by a three-litre engine, but revised to give 180bhp and a smooth flow of mid-range torque. This was the only unit offered for all markets, linked to a five-speed manual gearbox with a new clutch with a rubber insert (although the three-speed Sportomatic continued to be offered for a while, it was dropped in mid-1979).

The SC was available as a coupé or a Targa, with a body and interior very similar to that of the three-litre Carrera. There were, of course, a few detail changes, but without seeing the '911SC' badge on the tail, it took a connoisseur to tell the 1977 and 1978 model year machines apart.

As well as the new SC series, the 1977 Frankfurt Show also witnessed the debut of the 3299cc Turbo. The larger capacity was obtained via a slight increase in both bore and stroke, but with an air-to-air intercooler added to the specifications list, the fuel-injected unit now developed 300bhp in European trim (265bhp for the US). With an uprated four-speed manual gearbox, the latest Turbo was capable of speeds in excess of 160mph (255kph). Naturally, this level of performance called for superb brakes, and the Turbo had them in the form of four-pot calipers acting on ventilated and cross-drilled discs. However, one has to pay for racing technology, and by early 1978, the 911 Turbo commanded a mighty DM 79,900 – a far cry from the DM 21,900 asked for the very first 911s.

In competition, the 935/78 upheld Porsche's honour on the tracks, the 850bhp machine enabling the Stuttgart marque to hold onto its World Championship crown; the 935 also dominated the IMSA series in the States. Meanwhile, in the field of rallying, Jean-Pierre Nicolas won the 1978 Monte Carlo Rally in a 911, and Porsche came second on the Safari.

The evergreen 911
The 924 Turbo was introduced towards the end of 1978, giving rise to yet more rumours that the 911 was nearing the end of its reign. While the 928 was not selling at expected levels (due to current world economy rather than any failing in the car itself), the 924 Turbo filled the gap between the strict 924 and the larger, V8 machine, both in terms of price and speed – it was a touch cheaper than the 911SC coupé and offered a similar level of performance.

Despite this, the 911 series continued almost unchanged into the 1980 season, and helped Porsche retain its WCM and IMSA titles in 1979. For 1980, the European markets acquired a more powerful engine for the SC (rated at 188bhp), enhanced equipment levels, and a new exhaust system for the Turbo, readily distinguished by its twin pipes.

In America, the 1980 models came with a Lambda-sond sensor, improving efficiency by constantly varying the air/fuel mixture to give a more effective burn in the combustion chamber. Combined with a new three-way catalytic converter, emissions were also reduced, and the unit (Type 930/07) duly qualified for use in all 50 States.

On the other hand, the Turbo was dropped from the US line-up at the end of 1979, and would not return to that market until the 1986 season. The 935 racer had also run its course, with the 924 as the factory's weapon of choice in competition during 1980. Perhaps, at last, the 911 was being pushed into the background, although the rear-engined model still managed to shine in the IMSA and SCCA Trans-Am events, and took rally pilots to victory on the Tour de Corse and in the European Rally Championship.

Europeans were given another power hike for 1981 (taking maximum output up to 204bhp), silencing the critics who had often pointed out that the SC unit was down on power compared to the 200bhp Carrera of 1976-1977. With a new five-speed gearbox and re-adoption of a traditional clutch, detail changes were made to the suspension and interior, and European-spec cars also gained side indicator repeaters on the front wings. In the States, the engine remained unchanged, although US buyers did at least receive the latest transmission and suspension modifications.

Company politics
Ernst Fuhrmann, Porsche's Chairman and designer of the first Carrera

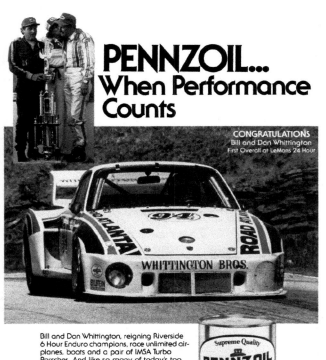

Advertising showing the 935 of Bill and Don Whittington. The Whittington brothers had a great deal of success at Le Mans (winning in 1979 with Klaus Ludwig in support), and in the America IMSA series.

engine, was eventually ousted from office in November 1980. Ferry Porsche later stated he felt Fuhrmann had trouble understanding the market (he did come from an engineering rather than commercial background, after all), but there was an underlying personality clash, too.

Peter Schutz became Chairman on 1 January 1981, hand-picked by Ferry Porsche. Born in Berlin in 1930, Schutz had spent most of his life in America before moving to the Deutz engineering concern in 1978 to take up the position of Director of Powertrain R&D.

Whereas Fuhrmann had almost dismissed the 911 in recent years, preferring to put the company's resources into the 928 and the forthcoming 944, Schutz made it his mission to revive the legendary air-cooled model and give it the development needed to keep it

A publicity picture taken for America's 1980 model year brochure. The 911SC coupé can be seen in the foreground, with the Targa version behind and to the left (although bright trim was actually abandoned for 1980). In the background, 928s line up behind the Targa, with the 924 and 924S making up the numbers.

competitive. Schutz went on record as saying: "So long as there's demand for a certain model, we'll go on making it." It was exactly what Porsche enthusiasts wanted to hear.

The Schutz era began promisingly, with a great deal of investment pumped into new production lines and a computerized parts centre at Zuffenhausen. Four-wheel drive was being assessed for the 911, which confirmed the new man's stated intention to keep the rear-engined car in the line-up, and the factory restoration shop did its first of many slant-nose conversions.

Based on the Turbo, the first slant-nose model was completed on 16 July 1981 (chassis number 619). With front bodywork resembling that of the early 935 racer (complete with low-mounted front lights and cooling vents), sill kit, wider rear arches (with air ducts for engine and brake cooling, plus the oil cooler which had been moved rearwards), and a traditional Turbo rear wing, it was built as a special order at this time, although the conversion was listed as an official factory option a few years later.

The 944
The gap between the 924 and 928 was narrowed for the 1982 model year by the appearance of the 2.5-litre, four-

cylinder 944. Although clearly based on the 924 both visually (there was a striking resemblance to the Carrera GT) and in mechanical layout, the 944 used less VW-Audi sourced parts, and was much quicker.

Although the 928 went into production with a 4.5-litre V8, the plans for the original engine proposed a five-litre unit. Basically, the 944 powerplant was half of that prototype V8. With a 2479cc displacement, it developed a healthy 163bhp, contra-rotating balance shafts helping to keep it smooth.

Writing for *Classic Cars*, Roger Bell noted at the time of the new model's UK launch: "So excellent are the qualities that really matter – performance, economy, refinement, comfort, build quality, finish – that the 944's few deficiencies seem rather trivial ... Even at £13,000, the five-speed manual does not appear to have a competitor in sight."

A new star at Frankfurt
The 1981 Frankfurt Show saw the debut of the 'Studie' concept car – Porsche's first true convertible since the mid-1960s. But the Studie, based on the Turbo body and running gear, was far more than just an attractive drophead, as it also featured four-wheel drive. Although 4WD was not adopted on production cars for some time, the 911SC Cabriolet, with its traditional wingline rather than the bulging metal of the Turbo, duly made an appearance at the 1982 Geneva Show and went on sale at the start of the 1983 season.

Meanwhile, a few revisions were made to the 1982 911 models, such as painted centres on the ATS alloys (to make them look like the Fuchs forged items), a new rear spoiler, and new markings on the gauges and switchgear.

For 1983, the SC was much the same, apart from the introduction of the Cabriolet, of course. This was because

a new normally-aspirated model was waiting in the wings, although the Turbo was given a new exhaust with a different wastegate outlet system, recalibrated Bosch injection and a stiffer crankcase. Power remained unchanged on the turbocharged car, but torque was increased to a healthy 317lbft.

The big news for 1984 for Porsche fans was the introduction of the four-wheel drive 959 supercar, first shown at the 1983 Frankfurt Show. The twin-turbo, 2.8-litre engine produced no less than 450bhp, endowing the six-speed Group B monster with a 0-60 time of 3.9 seconds and a top speed approaching 200mph (320kph). However, priced at DM 420,000 apiece, it was nearly ten times the price of a contemporary 944! For those in the real world on a realistic budget, the next best thing was a new Carrera ...

The Carrera name revived
Once again, Porsche used the Carrera

Publicity shot showing the American Carrera range in Cabriolet, Targa and coupé guises. Note the 'telephone dial' alloys on the Targa; this wheel was introduced with the Carrera series but discontinued at the end of the 1987 season.

35

appellation on the 911, but this time, rather than being applied to a short-run, thinly disguised racer, it was given to the standard normally-aspirated 911 range: the base model had progressed to such an extent that the marketing people had no qualms about using this legendary tag on the entry level 911.

Introduced in Frankfurt alongside the 959 concept vehicle, the NA 911 range acquired a 3.2-litre powerplant, said to be up to 80 per cent new. With a 3164cc capacity and the Bosch Motronic DME engine control system, the European-spec Type 930/20 unit delivered 231bhp, while the US version (with a catalytic converter and Lambda sensor) developed 207bhp at 5900rpm.

The Carrera continued with the three body variations of the SC initially, although, eventually, a so-called 'Turbo Look' body package (known as the Carrera Sport Package in Germany, or SE/Super Sport in the UK) was made available for NA coupés. This included Turbo body panels, the Turbo's uprated suspension and brakes, and the larger wheel and tyre combination. This option (number M491) naturally added weight (and aerodynamic drag) but no power, so was of cosmetic value only.

Featuring a new five-speed gearbox with a transmission oil cooler and uprated brakes behind a fresh alloy wheel design, these new Carrera models perfectly complemented the 3.3-litre Turbo. At the same time, the standard 928 was dropped in the reshuffle, with the higher powered 928S carrying the series mantle.

Performance was certainly not a dirty word in Zuffenhausen and Porsche engineers, for so long tied up with the Group C racers, gladly turned their attention to a new rally car – the three-litre 911SC/RS. As an evolution of the discontinued 911SC, only 20 were needed to meet homologation requirements, and the lightweight 255bhp machine had no shortage of buyers, despite its DM 188,100 price tag. The model did well in the Middle East Championship and the ERC, and Rene Metge won the 1984 Paris-Dakar event with a four-wheel drive 911. There was even a return to F1 at this time, as Porsche built the TAG engines which powered the contemporary McLarens.

End of an era

In the USA the long running marketing agreement – which had resulted in Porsches and Audis being sold alongside each other under the auspices of Volkswagen of America Inc – finally came to an end on 31 August 1984. From now on, Porsche was on its own, with offices in Reno, and a new distribution system that used 40 so-called 'Porsche Centres' across the States. Eventually, after a great deal of opposition from existing dealers, this innovative plan was watered down somewhat, and, amidst all the upheaval, American sales fell slightly in 1984, down from 21,831 to 19,611 units.

For 1985, Americans received a 32v five-litre version of the 928S, rated at 288bhp. By summer 1986, this model was offered in all markets, now known as the Series 4 and with a useful 320bhp on tap, giving the luxury GT a top speed approaching 170mph (272kph).

Meanwhile, while the 944 Turbo was making its debut in mid-1985, production of the two-litre 924 came to an end. With it disappeared the last real vestiges of VW-Audi content in a Porsche car, although the model did continue for a short while in 924S guise, powered by the 944 engine. The much talked-about small Porsche, intended to slot into the range below the 924 (and possibly available in coupé, Targa and convertible forms), simply failed to materialize ...

The 911 story continues

A spokesman for the company stated there would be heavy investment in the Zuffenhausen facility, allowing production to increase from 80 to 120 cars per day over the following year or so. Ironically, most of this extra capacity was allocated not to the 928, but to the 911, now practically guaranteed another ten years without major change.

For 1985, the Carrera's fuel tank capacity was increased to 85 litres (18.7 Imperial gallons), oil cooling was improved, and gearshift travel slightly reduced. Inside, a new four-spoke steering wheel was adopted, and power adjustments were provided on the revised front seats. The Turbo inherited the latest steering wheel and seats, and also gained central locking,

heater elements in the seats, and a modified brake master cylinder to reduce pedal effort.

The 1986 model year was quite significant, as the Turbo returned to America (with 282bhp SAE), the 'Turbo Look' body and chassis package became available on all NA cars, a power top became available on the Cabriolet (standard for 1987), and the dashboard received its first major revision since 1964. There were also a few suspension changes, and wider wheels for the Turbo.

Incidentally, European versions of the slant-nose Turbo were now fitted with tuned engines developing no less than 330bhp. The UK listed this model as standard during 1986, although it wasn't until the 1987 season that it was sold worldwide as a proper production car.

Meanwhile, Germany's latest emissions regulations came into force in January 1986, stipulating a requirement that all new vehicles use three-way catalytic converters to avoid a hefty pollution tax. It was an interesting development, but the lack of unleaded fuel in many other parts of Europe made rather a mockery of it, and it was no coincidence that a 'cat' equipped 911 had cost over DM 2000 more than one without in the 1985 season. With so many cars staying in Germany for home market consumption, though, the issue was just as important to Porsche as changes in Federal legislation for the majority of sports car manufacturers.

The 959 project

The 959 had been announced at the 1983 Frankfurt Show (as the 'Gruppe B'), but it was not until September 1986 that deliveries of the first 250 (increased from the original 200) production cars were scheduled. Ironically, the works rally raid entries had come to an end following a convincing victory on the 1986 Paris-Dakar, Group B rallying had ended (the 1987 season was campaigned by Group A machines) and, although the Type 961 was being developed, most of the serious, high budget racing teams were competing in Group C.

Anyway, with a bore and stroke of 95 x 67mm, the flat-six had a capacity of 2848cc. With an 8.0:1 compression ratio, Bosch MP-Jetronic

The 959 supercar, seen here (from left to right) in Paris-Dakar rally raid guise, in its production road car form, and as the Type 961 racer. Very few were built, although the Group B project did provide Porsche engineers with a lot of useful data and experience which was later put to good use on the 911 series.

fuel-injection, and twin, water-cooled sequential turbos (a feature unique at that time for a road car) and intercoolers, the 959 engine developed 450bhp at 6500rpm.

The six-speed gearbox transferred power to a computer-controlled, variable split four-wheel drive system with four switchable modes. This virtually killed the undesirable handling traits associated with the 911 since birth; the throttle could be closed during cornering with only a trace of oversteer instead of a vicious swing of the tail. Suspension was via double wishbones all-round, with a computer-controlled ride height system acting on a pair of gas dampers in each corner.

The body, more swoopy and aerodynamic than that of the 911, had a steel monocoque, but the bolt-on panels were either aluminium, polyurethane, carbonfibre or Kevlar. With a bonded-in windscreen and no rain gutters, it had a Cd figure of just 0.31 with zero lift, and, thanks to the lightweight materials employed, the whole thing weighed in at 1450kg (3190lb) in standard trim, or 1350kg (2970lb) in ultra-rare Sport guise.

The Sport was lighter thanks to deletion of the automatic ride height system, air conditioning, rear seats, some of the soundproofing, and the passenger side door mirror, and by replacing the standard front seats with lightweight versions. Otherwise, the interior would have been quite familiar to the driver of a 1986 911, apart from the 340kph speedo and torque split indicator in place of the clock.

Including prototypes, ultimately, a total of 283 959s were produced (1987 chassis numbers account for 254), the vast majority of them built to standard specification rather than the lightweight Sport option.

In its review of the 959, *MotorSport* made an interesting observation: "The Porsche 959 is an enormously competent car which represents great investment, both in terms of engineering expertise and customer investment. Were all this to be done for merely 250 customers it would, unquestionably, have been a folly of the grandest proportions, but of course that is not Porsche's way. This is the pot pourri of technical exercises that will be applied to the range over

the next ten years. Nothing goes to waste at Weissach ..."

The 1987 model year

For 1987, the Carrera was given a new five-speed gearbox with a hydraulically actuated clutch, along with a few suspension modifications to suit the Getrag unit's installation, wider front tyres, and a revised rear reflector. At the same time, America received a more powerful engine, rated at 217bhp, and fell into line with European-style headlights.

In February 1987, Porsche announced Targa and Cabriolet versions of the Turbo, and the slant-nose conversion became an official option thereafter, available on all three body variations. Sales began in Germany and America during spring that year, although the UK had to wait until the 1988 season for these latest additions to the range.

Porsche had recently shown a number of interesting developments based on the 911, but 1988 saw official confirmation that plans to produce a two-seater costing under $20,000 had been dropped as far as production in Germany was concerned

The Turbo had been available in coupé form only for many years. All that changed in the spring of 1987 with the introduction of Targa and Cabriolet versions.

– the state of world currency exchange rates meant it was simply not a viable proposition. In addition, the stock market crash of October 1987 would have a devastating affect on car sales.

Meanwhile, by the end of the 1987 model year, over 250,000 six-cylinder 911s had been built, along with 32,399 four-cylinder 912s. In all, including prototypes, 284,803 cars from the 911 series had been produced, and there was still a lot of life in it yet ...

The 1988 season
The biggest change for 1988 was the adoption of 15-inch Fuchs alloys as standard on the Carrera, signifying the end of the so-called 'telephone dial' wheels for the 911. All 911s received more equipment as standard, although one particular model had less ...

By now, the 911 range was very extensive, with standard and Turbo Look versions of the three main body types, slant-nose models, and a choice of two extremely refined powerplants, available with up to 330bhp in some cases. However, prices had increased dramatically over the years, and some of the raw appeal of the original models had been lost. Enter the Club Sport.

Introduced to the public at the 1987 Frankfurt Show, the so-called Club Sport model was a Carrera specified with option M637, which reduced weight by around 70kg (155lb) by deleting a number of items. Mechanically, the Club Sport had a higher rev limit, although power output remained at 231bhp. Although there wasn't a badge on the engine lid, fancy graphics, aping those of earlier

lightweight 911s, were listed as an option.

Porsche prices continued to rise, however, about DM 6000 up on 1987 model year levels at the start of the season, before a further increase in the spring of 1988. The increases were made partly to cover the cost of a new body plant, which opened at Zuffenhausen in 1988 – it cost the company DM 125,000,000 ...

Still, although 959 production was due to end in mid-1988, Schutz expected Porsche prices to continue climbing rather than decrease – the marque was going even further upmarket. Daily production at Zuffenhausen was around 102 days per day at the start of the 1988 model year (a good 75 per cent of these being 911s), with NSU's old Neckarsulm

The dashboard had received its first major revision since the 911's introduction for the 1986 season. This picture shows the interior of the 1987 model year Turbo for the US market. The stereo is a Blaupunkt Reno unit, by the way.

plant producing the four-cylinder 924s and 944s.

Boardroom drama

In America, sales of all German cars suffered in 1987. Although figures for the 924S, for instance, were down by only 3 per cent compared with 1986, this was actually a disaster, as the model was sold for only half of that year. The main reason for this poor showing was the strong deutschmark, the value of which had increased by 23 per cent against the dollar in just 12 months.

At the end of 1987, in the wake of dwindling profits (although the currencies had shifted 23 per cent, prices in the States would only bear a 14 per cent increase), a press release stated: "The Supervisory Board of Dr Ing. h. c. F. Porsche AG has announced that Mr Peter W. Schutz and Porsche AG have mutually agreed that Mr Schutz will resign from his position

as Chairman of the Executive Board effective 31 December 1987.

"Mr Heinz Branitzki, Deputy Chairman of the Executive Board since 1976, was elected by the Supervisory Board yesterday [16 December] to be the new Chairman of the Executive Board as of 1 January 1988."

Schutz was determined to save the 911, which he did very successfully, but he also allowed the company to become almost dependent on the American market. Although the US market had always been immensely important, Ferry Porsche had quite deliberately kept its share of production under 50 per cent, as he didn't want to rely too heavily on sales in one country. Over 60 per cent of production was destined for America by the end of Schutz's tenure, and, with an unfavourable exchange rate, this was a disastrous situation which happened to coincide with the stock

market crash, an additional problem for the luxury car maker.

As for world economy, no-one could blame Schutz for that – it's worth noting that the events of October 1987, at least in percentage terms, were twice as bad of those of the Wall Street Crash of the late 1920s. And we all know what that led to ... Although the future looked grim, Ferry Porsche was positive there was still a market for the Stuttgart thoroughbreds.

Interestingly, rumours of Schutz's departure had been circulating around the industry for some time, and in some quarters Ferdinand Piech was being suggested as a possible replacement. Ironically, despite his close links with Porsche through previous experience and family bloodlines (as the son of Ferry Porsche's sister), Piech was officially made Chairman of Audi on the same day as Branitzki took up his new position.

In America, as part of a major management shake-up in the US operation, Brian Bowler was given the post of PCNA's new President, but in reality John Cook (the ex-BMW of North America boss who had headed the Reno office since its inception) could hardly be blamed for the poor exchange rates and the general downturn in world economy. The outlook was bleak in the UK, too. Following Black Monday and the subsequent demise of the Yuppie, the question was how much longer could Porsche trade on its name?

959 update & a new 4WD car

As noted earlier, deliveries of the 959 supercar began at the start of the 1987 model year, much later than originally expected, although the model still managed to generate a great deal of enthusiasm in the press. Higher than expected numbers were built: including the prototypes, a total of 283 959s had been produced by the time the last one rolled out of the Zuffenhausen workshops in mid-1988.

The 944 was developing into an accomplished performance car. This is the 1987 model year 944S, which featured a 16-valve head.

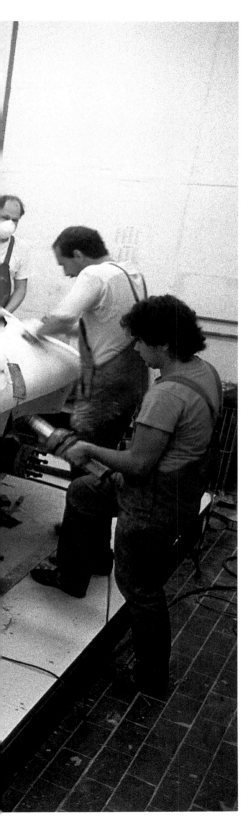

The 1989 Panamericana showcar slowly taking shape in the Porsche workshops. Its styling would point the way towards the future.

Most were standard cars, as opposed to the lighter Sport specification, and most were built in 1987.

The people at the EPA and DOT ensured the 959 would not be sold in the States in its original guise. But instead of bowing to the legislators, the men at Zuffenhausen decided it was not worth going to the trouble of certifying the model, especially in view of demand elsewhere, which was sufficient to guarantee homologation.

The 959 continued to be listed for some time after production ended. Indeed, its picture and specifications appeared in the UK's 1988 Motor Show catalogue – the real thing, finished in metallic grey was on the PCGB stand.

Meanwhile, in its issue dated 4 May 1988, *Autocar* published a photograph of a new Carrera and its 4WD drivetrain, noting that domestic sales would begin in September. The Carrera 4 was the perfect way to mark the 25th anniversary of the 911; its extra weight was overcome by giving the car more power – 250bhp from a 3.6-litre version of the familiar flat-six.

The Carrera 4 went on sale alongside the other 911s for the 1989 season, but the whole rear-engined range duly adopted this facelifted body and new engine over the next year or so, receiving the Type 964 designation along the way.

Matters of the moment

The 924S disappeared at the end of the 1988 season. Was another 'cheap' model the way forward? A Porsche official noted: "It's a vicious circle. We want to build an affordable sports car. That means big volume and lots of proprietary parts. But as soon as you do that, the quality and prestige of the products suffer. We learned our lesson with the old Volks-Porsche 914, and with the original 924. Today, the management won't accept any car unless it's 100 per cent Porsche."

Although prototypes were built, the level of investment needed to get such a project off the ground – not just in terms of R&D, but also the requirement for a new factory to handle the level of production necessary to make it viable – simply didn't make commercial sense. A deciding factor was the strong deutschmark; having been around 3.5 DM to $1 at the start of 1985, three years later it stood at less than 1.7 DM. In this price sensitive end of the market, too many compromises would have had to be made to keep costs down. In 1988 official confirmation came that plans had been dropped to produce a two-seater costing less than $20,000, at least as far as production in Germany was concerned.

As the deutschmark continued to strengthen, Porsche decided to adopt a policy of going even more upmarket – unfortunately, in order to see any kind of profit on cheaper models, prices in export markets had risen to such an extent that the cars were rendered uncompetitive. Although, for the vast majority, the decision to concentrate on the top end of the market took away the chance to realize a dream of Porsche ownership, in reality, it was the only logical answer.

Helmuth Bott, Porsche's technical supremo, retired in September 1988. Professor Bott was replaced as Technical Director by Dr Ulrich Bez. At the same time, whilst Tony Lapine remained head of styling, it was announced that Horst Marchart had been made responsible for road car development, and Rainer Srock was put in charge of the Weissach facility.

Branitzki had become Chairman following the departure of Peter Schutz, but he wanted to retire. Having done a sterling job in a difficult situation, eventually, in March 1990, Branitzki managed to hand over the reins to Arno Bohn, a young high-flyer who'd made his name in the computer world.

Competition news

The WSPC was dominated by Group C machinery, but at least the Joest Porsche team came third at Le Mans in 1988 to keep the marque in the public eye. In America, although Porsche won the IMSA GTP title (its top driver came third), the Indycar project was not a success – a fourth place in Nazareth being the best showing in the March-Porsche's first full season.

In the 1989 World Sports-Prototype Championship, the Joest and Brun teams trailed the Sauber-

Two legendary names came together for 1989 to form the Carrera Speedster.

The Porsche line-up for the 1990 season, with 911 variants to the left, the 928 in the centre, and 944-based models on the right. As can be seen in the photograph, the 964-type 911 was available in coupé, Targa and Cabriolet guises by this time.

The 964-based Turbo was introduced at the 1990 Geneva Show, although sales did not officially begin until September that year.

Mercedes outfit. In America, the 911 drivers kept a low profile in the SCCA and IMSA events (Nissan won the GTP title), and the CART Indy programme simply yielded yet more disappointment. Although there was a win at Mid-Ohio and a few pole positions were captured over the season, thus offering a glint of hope, fans had a right to expect more from the legendary Stuttgart marque.

The 1989 season
While the 3.3-litre turbocharged engine remained the same for the 1989 season, the Turbo at last gained a five-speed gearbox (a four-speed unit had been a feature of the Turbo since introduction), and there were a few suspension changes for the turbocharged car, too. There were no engine or suspension changes for the Carrera, although the Fuchs wheel rim diameter was increased.

The 911 Speedster was first displayed at the 1987 Frankfurt Show, and eventually went on sale in January 1989. Essentially a Carrera Cabriolet specified with the M503 option, the Speedster had a cut-down windscreen, frameless side windows, and a manually-operated lightweight hood that was usually hidden by a composite material cover.

The Speedster was lighter than the Cabriolet (largely due to a stripped out interior), and could be specified with the Turbo Look body. Available from January to September 1989 only, a total of 2065 were built.

And so we come to the end of another era. In fact, the new era had already dawned in the shape of the Type 964, and this had two distinct consequences: some were happy to wait for new variations due in the 1990 season, whilst others scrabbled to secure one of the last of the 'classic' Porsches ...

The 964 series
The Carrera 4 coupé had already been on sale for a year before the rear-wheel drive Carrera 2 version made its debut in time for the 1990 season. With its 3.6-litre engine, revised suspension system and face-lifted body (its larger, more rounded bumpers giving a more modern interpretation of the 911 theme), it signalled the end of the 3.2-litre Carreras and their Turbo stablemate. As before, the new Carreras were available in coupé, Targa and Cabriolet guises.

January 1990 saw the launch of the Tiptronic transmission – an automatic gearbox far superior to the old Sportomatic, as it offered a fully automatic mode and two types of manual override: a traditional gear hold facility, and a +/- selector that allowed the driver to shift up or down by knocking the gearlever forward or backward. Popular from the outset, the idea was further enhanced in the 1995 model year by adding selector switches on the steering wheel.

Meanwhile, a new Turbo made its debut at the 1990 Geneva Show. This was basically a stopgap model, with the 964 body and an engine given a few tweaks in order to extract 320bhp from 3.3 litres – 20bhp more than the previous European-spec unit could muster. The new five-speed Turbo officially went on sale in September 1990.

There were no major changes in the 964 range after that, although the Gulf War hurt sales of luxury sports cars worldwide, and America slipped into recession. The amiable Frederick J. Schwab was now PCNA's new President, and he certainly had an uphill battle on his hands.

A new RS
A new Carrera RS was launched in the summer of 1991 (although a prototype had been displayed at the NEC near Birmingham at the end of 1990), reviving a legendary name in the process. Along with an aluminium front lid and thinner glass, the interior was stripped out to reduce weight, and, combined with another 10bhp at the wheels, gave the car livelier response and handling. There was a Sport and Touring version, and a run of competition models, including a batch for the Carrera Cup one-make series.

On the subject of motorsport, Porsche returned to the F1 arena at around this time (after an approach from Footwork in February 1990); quite surprising, given its poor performance in the American CART Indy series – at least compared with the German manufacturer's usual standard.

This time, however, the situation was a little riskier as the 3.5-litre V12 cam covers proudly carried Porsche insignia, setting the Zuffenhausen concern firmly in the spotlight, and the Footwork Arrows chassis it was destined to be installed in was certainly a lot less competitive than that of the McLaren.

Early testing was marred by a series of problems, and, sadly, things didn't improve on the track. Early hopes for 700bhp at 14,000rpm by the end of the first season were dashed (official figures quoted 650bhp at 12,000rpm), and the unit was found to be far too heavy to be competitive. This was a very disappointing chapter in Porsche history; the only finishes recorded during 1991 were when the Footwork chassis was fitted with a Cosworth engine, and even then no points were scored. In the end, the joint project was formally abandoned on the eve of the Japanese Grand Prix, and the Footwork equipe signed up with Mugen-Honda for 1992.

The 968

Prototype pictures of the 968 began to appear in magazines during mid-1991.

It looked very similar to the 944, but disguise panels around the headlights and tail kept the final details out of reach of the long lens brigade until the car was launched at that year's Frankfurt Show.

Mechanically similar to the 944 S2, the 968 was powered by a development of the four-cylinder S2 unit, and linked to either a Getrag six-speed manual or four-speed Tiptronic semi-automatic gearbox. The three-litre, twin-cam 16v engine featured 'Variocam' (Porsche's variable inlet valve timing system), pushing power up to 240bhp.

Like the 944, the 968 was available in both closed coupé and cabriolet forms. The body styling, executed by Harm Laagay (now head of Porsche's styling department following Tony Lapine's retirement), was a cross between the 944 and 928, although 80 per cent of the panelwork was new.

More 964 models

A Carrera 2 Turbo Look Cabriolet was launched at the 1991 Frankfurt Show, and the States received a 911 America Roadster based on this vehicle. Even this limited edition model could do nothing to halt the downward spiral of US sales, though, reduced to just 4133 units (all Porsches) for 1992, prompting the cancellation of a proposed American Carrera Cup race series. Japan became Porsche's third biggest market at this time, and became increasingly important for the Stuttgart marque as the years passed.

Another new 911 appeared at the 1992 Geneva Show – the Turbo S. This was given a more powerful engine and a lighter body, although very few were ever built. In addition, the US market received the RS America, a milder version of the European RS that was able to clear the Federal regulations in place at that time.

Two new models were announced in October 1992 – the 3.6-litre Turbo, and the C2 Speedster. However, it would be a few months before either went into production, and both were ultimately classed as early 1994 models. The 360bhp Turbo was an impressive machine, although the concept, like that of the Speedster, was very familiar to Porsche followers.

Another RS/RSR series was launched at this time, powered by a 3746cc engine housed in a Turbo Look body. The Turbo Look body was also employed for a limited edition 'Celebration' coupé, built to commemorate the 30th anniversary of the world's favourite sports car.

Zuffenhausen blues

Porsche bid farewell to Arno Bohn at the end of 1992, together with 1850 factory workers (around 20 per cent of the staff) as the company hit hard times. Bohn had struggled to fit in with the old regime in Stuttgart, and his place in the Chairman's office was taken by Porsche's production specialist, Wendelin Wiedeking.

Italian advertising from early 1993, showing the 968, 911 and 928. A face-lifted 911 was introduced that year, giving the classic air-cooled model more of a 'family look' to match its stablemates.

Faced with a record loss of DM 239,000,000, Wiedeking made it his mission to cut costs by up to a third within three years, a policy that would affect both white- and blue-collar jobs (not to mention setting the axe in motion on the eight-cylinder Type 989 four-door saloon project), but, long-term, it was the only way forward.

Interestingly, Ulrich Bez, who had replaced Helmuth Bott on his retirement, also departed from the scene. Bez's office at Weissach was now occupied by Horst Marchart – a proper Porsche man who'd joined the company in 1960.

In the background, East and West Germany had come together at the end of 1989 with the fall of the Berlin Wall, but financial problems associated with the reunification (made official in October 1990) were making themselves felt. With Porsche relying on home sales almost as much as those in the States, this was another difficult issue for the company to deal with.

End of the line

The 993 coupé was unveiled at the 1993 Frankfurt Show, meaning that the days were numbered for the 964 series. Some models soldiered on into the 1994 season, but soon the 993 range would take on the hallowed 911 mantle. The 928 and 968 were still available, but a new concept car, unveiled at the 1993 Detroit Show, sent the rumour mill into overdrive. This pretty little mid-engined two-seater was christened the 'Boxster,' although it would be several years before a production version appeared, and, even then, it was quite different to the car displayed in the States.

A truly modern 911

The 993 series was much more than a simple face-lift – it was virtually a new car. The basic profile was retained, but the shape was far smoother; more aerodynamic, and thoroughly modern. The headlights sloped backward to give the car a new 'family look' frontal appearance, bringing the 911's styling in line with its 928 and 968 stablemates. Inside was a blend of old and new. The fascia was similar to that of the 964 cars, but seating and door panel designs were new.

Motive power was provided by a modified 964 unit that delivered 272bhp. It was mated to either a new six-speed manual gearbox or the optional four-speed Tiptronic, with drive going to the rear wheels only on the first cars, which inherited the Carrera nametag. A limited-slip differential and ABD could be specified at extra cost on this model, but came as standard on the four-wheel drive Carrera 4 version introduced for the 1995 season.

The suspension was also noteworthy, as a multi-link system (derived from that of the 928 and designed for the stillborn 989 saloon) was adopted for the rear, while the set-up at the front was carried over with a few minor revisions.

Thanks to Wiedeking's purge on production costs and the introduction of Japanese-style working practices, the new Carrera took 40 hours per car less to build. At the same time, quality was improved, and the 'just-in-time' system (dictating that parts were ordered and delivered as they were needed) helped ease cashflow and saved on valuable space at the Zuffenhausen plant. Introduced at

The 993 series kept the classic 911 profile, but was a far more modern interpretation of the theme. The chassis was also updated to improve handling, and make the car more refined and user-friendly.

DM 125,760, the new Carrera coupé was joined by a Cabriolet in March 1994 (no Targa at this stage).

Ironically, given that the 911 was to have been replaced on numerous occasions during its three decades of sales, in early 1995, 911 production was increased to 92 cars per day (up from 86), as the number of 968s being built was reduced, and 928 production was cut from four cars per day to just two! By this time, the last of the 964-based models had long since disappeared.

For 1995, as well as the introduction of a new C4 model, the Tiptronic transmission was upgraded to Tiptronic S specification, with selector switches added to the steering wheel. In March that year, a new four-wheel drive Turbo made its debut, powered by a twin-turbo 3.6-litre unit that developed no less than 408bhp. As before, the Turbo had a wider body, although only the rear wings were enlarged on the 180mph (288kph) 993-based model.

The GT2 & RS

The GT2 was a Turbo-based road-racer with a stripped out interior and a 430bhp version of the turbocharged flat-six (this engine could also be specified for European Turbos as an option). The road car went on sale in April 1995, by which time a 3.8-litre RS based on the NA car had made its debut. The 300bhp RS powerplant was the first 911 engine to feature what Porsche called 'Varioram,' which enhanced low- to mid-range torque by altering the length of the intake tract. Both cars excelled in the BPR Global Endurance GT series, which did a grand job of reviving the European GT scene, and with the introduction of a GT1 model for the 1996 season, Porsche was once again competing and winning at the top level in motorsport.

The 1996 model year

Ironically, given that it was intended to replace the 911 around 15 years earlier, the 928 failed to appear in the 1996 MY line-up, as did the shortlived

1. Manuel Reuter (D), Alexander Wurz (A), Davy Jones (USA)
Joest-Racing, Joest-Porsche, 354 Runden **(Gesamtsieger)**
2. Hans-Joachim Stuck (A), Thierry Boutsen (B), Bob Wollek (F)
Porsche AG, Porsche 911 GT1, 353 Runden - **(Sieger der Klasse GT1)**
3. Yannick Dalmas (F), Karl Wendlinger (A), Scott Goodyear (CAN)
Porsche AG, Porsche 911 GT1, 341 Runden
4. Lindsay Owen-Jones (GB), Pierre-Henri Raphanel (F), David Brabham (AUS)
West Competition, McLaren-BMW GTR F1 LM, 337 Runden
5. John Nielsen (DK), Thomas Bscher (D), Peter Kox (NL)
Gulf Racing, McLaren-BMW GTR F1 LM, 335 Runden
6. Andy Wallace (GB), Olivier Grouillard (F), Derek Bell (GB)
Harrods Mach One Racing, McLaren-BMW GTR F1 LM, 328 Runden
7. Henri Pescarolo (F), Franck Lagorge (F), Emmanuel Collard (F)
La Filière, Courage-Porsche, 327 Runden
8. Nelson Piquet (BR), Johnny Cecotto (YV), Danny Sullivan (USA)
Team Bigazzi SRL, McLaren-BMW GTR F1 LM, 324 Runden
9. Ray Bellm (GB), James Weaver (GB), J.J. Lehto (FIN)
Gulf Racing, McLaren-BMW GTR F1 LM, 323 Runden
10. Price Cobb (USA), Mark Dismore (USA), Shawn Hendricks (USA)
Canaska Southwind Motor, Chrysler Viper GTS-R, 320 Runden
11. Jacques Laffite (F), Steve Soper (GB), Marc Duez (B)
Team Bigazzi SRL, McLaren-BMW GTR F1 LM, 318 Runden
12. Guy Martinolle (F), Ralf Kelleners (D), Bruno Eichmann (CH)
Roock-Racing-Team, Porsche 911 GT2, 317 Runden - **(Sieger der Klasse GT2)**

LE MANS '96

Porsche triumphiert zum 14. Mal

PORSCHE

968. Although a few water-cooled models were sold in 1996 (leftover stock), officially, this left just the 911 in Porsche showrooms until the Boxster arrived. To try and fill the gaps a couple of new 911s were added to the line-up with the advent of the T-Serie. When the 1995 Frankfurt Show opened its doors, on display was a new Targa, a Carrera 4S variant, and a redesigned normally-aspirated engine.

The Targa bore little resemblance to its namesake of years gone by,

having a full-length glass sunroof that retracted inside the rear screen. The C4S was basically a four-wheel drive Turbo Look model, and, like the Targa and all the other Carreras, came with an uprated engine. With Varioram, bigger valves and a number of other refinements, the M64/05 unit now delivered 285bhp DIN at 6100rpm, along with 251lbft of torque.

On 15 July, the one millionth Porsche rolled off the line – a Carrera for the Swabian police force. Ultimately,

Porsche built around 21,000 911s in 1996, a record for the model, despite having been launched over 30 years earlier. Although the 911 had changed dramatically in this time, the concept had remained exactly the same ...

Links with a Stuttgart neighbour

In early 1992, rumours again surfaced of a cheaper convertible and coupé, supposedly priced significantly lower than the 968. Some even suggested a link between the drophead model and Mercedes-Benz: a suggestion quickly dismissed as rubbish by the venerable Paul Frere, who had a closer relationship than most with staff at the Zuffenhausen factory.

The Boxster arrived in late 1996 (making its debut at the 1996 Paris Show ready for the 1997 model year), but a price tag of $40,000 meant it could hardly be classed as cheap. At that time, a closed version was not planned. Frere's comments were proved correct as the months passed; not surprising, really, given that the management wanted Porsche to remain a specialist rather than a volume producer.

There was, however, a link between Porsche and Mercedes-Benz, with the two companies sharing convertible roof technology and Porsche planning to badge-engineer the M-Class SUV. Eventually, in January 1997, this idea fell through,

although Porsche did later introduce the Cayenne – a luxury SUV developed jointly with Volkswagen.

A final fling

For 1997, the Carrera S was added to the 911 range (a Turbo Look version of the strict Carrera), joined later by a limited edition 430bhp Turbo S. The GT1 road car also went on sale, although at DM 1,550,000, it was always going to be a rarity. The 993 series soldiered on into the 1998 season, but a new 911 had made its debut at the 1997 Frankfurt Show, signalling the end of the air-cooled era. From now on, all new Porsches would be water-cooled ...

The 1998 model year line-up, with 993-based 911s flanking the new water-cooled Carrera (centre of the front row), and the mid-engined Boxster (behind the 996 model).

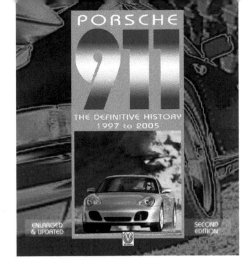

3

The 996 series

The 1997 Frankfurt Show brought with it a new era in Porsche history, for this event marked the debut of the first water-cooled 911 – the Type 996 ...

As well as rumours of a V12 supercar, predictions in the early 1990s pointed toward a V6 or V8 for the new 911 (Type 996). This was probably a fair assumption, as the V8-engined 989 looked like a bigger version of the 996, and to share technology would have been an obvious way to save on production costs.

At this point in the story it's worth including a few words on the 4.5-litre 989. Tail styling was indeed

Although accurate pictures were appearing in a number of magazines, such as Autobild, as early as the summer of 1995, official 996 photographs were not released until quite close to its launch. This is one of a series of pictures issued by the factory in July 1997.

a big mistake. As Professor Ferdinand Porsche was once told: "Shoemaker, stick to your trade." Porsche's trade was building sports cars for the connoisseur.

With the 989 axed and the 928 discontinued, the new 911 – once again carrying the Carrera name tag – was ultimately powered by a traditional flat-six, but no longer featuring air cooling: the new engine was a water-cooled 3.4-litre six, based on that of the 2.5-litre Boxster unit.

The switch to water-cooling allowed Porsche to easily comply with noise and exhaust regulations, which were becoming increasingly difficult to satisfy with the old air-cooled units. It also made it easier to use four-valve per cylinder technology to boost performance and cut emissions and fuel consumption. The 24v engine, with twin-cams on each bank, developed a healthy 300bhp.

Transmission and chassis details were refined, but pretty much carried over in principle, with a six-speed manual or Tiptronic automatic, although the latter was given a fifth gear for the new 911.

The 996 prototype had longer headlights, running further back towards the screen, and not as wide as those used for production; the rear end was flatter, too. But when the 996 was introduced on stand 56 at the 1997 Frankfurt Show, it became clear that 40 per cent of its parts were shared with the Boxster, the main reason for adopting a new 911 body style so soon after the successful 993 had hit the marketplace – economy of scale.

There was also the embarrassing fact that the Boxster was larger (longer and wider) than the 2+2 993 Carrera! This did not look good in the showroom, so the new Carrera would, in effect, replace the old 911 and the 928. As *MotorSport* observed, the new car was "more of a world-beating sports GT than a true replacement for

exceptionally similar to that of the 996, but, combined with a longer wheelbase, the C-pillar was slimmer to allow more space for the rear doors. The front mask was essentially the same as that of the 993, but with the indicator/side light unit closer to the headlamp on each side. The overall shape was actually very elegant, the window graphics and roofline at the

back balancing the design perfectly, albeit at the cost of some rear passenger headroom.

No less than $90,000,000 was spent on the front-engined 989 project, which duly came to nothing. In reality, though, it could have cost the company dearly in the long run – to go head-to-head with Mercedes-Benz, BMW and Audi could have been

Harm Lagaay and Pinky Lai discussing design details on the far side of a styling buck, while clay modellers refine the shape as they speak. Lai (picked out in this shot as the only one with black hair) sketched the original concept drawings for the 996.

Wendelin Wiedeking (born in Germany in August 1952) turned around the business fortunes of Porsche following the departure of Arno Bohn from the President's office. The new 911 and Boxster were key components in Wiedeking's strategic plan to raise profits through greater productivity, and reduce delivery times.

A team photo to celebrate a job well done. Marchart and Lagaay – head of road car development and head of styling respectively – can be seen to the right of this shot.

the 911." This really was a brand new 911, not simply a face-lifted version of the original.

Importance of the 996

There will always be those who will lament the passing of the air-cooled generation, but Porsche had to move with the times. Wendelin Wiedeking, who headed the Stuttgart company,

knew only too well that survival in the highly competitive world that is the motor industry called for drastic measures.

Wiedeking quickly realized that the old 911s were costing too much to build, with this additional expense being passed on to the customer. By reducing material costs by 40 per cent, and instilling the same

'lean thinking' philosophy amongst major suppliers to further reduce production costs, efficiency – and thus profit – could be increased, allowing greater investment in new model lines.

The 996 and 986 (Boxster) were confirmed internally as Porsche's future production lines early in 1992. Both were developed at the same

Horst Marchart, who had been with Porsche since 1960, was a man moulded in Bott's image; together with Wiedeking, the Vienna-born enthusiast, set about putting the company on the road to recovery. After his sterling work on the 993, Bernd Kahnau was charged with heading the 996 programme under Marchart.

Born in Holland in December 1946, Harm Lagaay (responsible for the design of the 924, and returning to Zuffenhausen in 1989 after spells with Ford Europe and BMW), was appointed head of the Porsche styling department following Tony Lapine's retirement.

time to minimize costs, with Rainer Srock in charge of co-ordinating the programmes; many parts were shared for the same reason. Development and tooling costs amounted to around DM 1.5 billion for the Boxster and new 911 combined – a lot of money, granted, but a lot less than most modern automobiles cost to bring to market, and an investment that ultimately secured the future independence of Porsche at a time when so many smaller manufacturers were either falling by the wayside or being gobbled up by larger concerns.

Wiedeking, who had made all the right decisions up to this point in the proceedings, would have to wait and see if this new direction of water-cooled engines and shared platforms was the right one, but it was certainly a brave move bringing half a century of history to a sudden end. Of course, the air-cooled Porsche had been living on borrowed time for years – one only

has to read the earlier chapters in this book to appreciate that!

The production body

Harm Lagaay (responsible for the design of the 924 and returning to Zuffenhausen in 1989 after spells with Ford Europe and BMW) was appointed head of Porsche's styling department following Tony Lapine's retirement. As such, Lagaay was in charge of the Type 996 design work – a huge undertaking given the legendary status of the 911 series, but one he relished, having an able team, including Wolfgang Mobius and Pinky Lai, to back him up.

Commenting on why the 911 had remained so popular for so many years, Lagaay said: "I like to think of the 911 as the eternal mistress. You always keep her, no matter what the state of your marriage. You want to have her physically, but it's also a meeting of minds. The 911 is the same. It's more than just owning the car, for it offers

eternal interest, the intrigue never fades, and there is always something new to discover. And our new mistress is even better."

From the front, only the air intakes distinguished the 996 from the Boxster. The front structure, wings, luggage compartment lid and lighting units were all the same, but the front bumper (a large, one-piece moulded section) was quite different, with the 911 featuring a full-width intake below a smaller one on each side of the area reserved for the number plate.

The Boxster's fuel lid was the opposite side to the 993 and earlier 911s, although, due to the shared front structure with the 986, the 996 also adopted this new location, giving access to a 65-litre (14.3 imperial gallon) tank; both the Boxster and the 996 lost the washer filler neck alongside the fuel filler (a feature on 911s since 1973), the reservoir now located in the nearside corner near the bulkhead, next to the 80Ah battery, also situated in front of the bulkhead on the new generation cars. Incidentally, the fuel lid worked in conjunction with the central locking, so no longer required a separate release.

The door skins were also the same as the Boxster's. Actually, the steel used on the 996 (and the Boxster) was rather unusual in that it was pressed in varying thicknesses. This had the effect of reducing weight in areas that were not load bearing, as they could be made thinner, as well as adding strength in selected areas through a thicker gauge material.

The front screen had a five-degree steeper rake than previous 911s, resulting in a modified roofline. Side windows sat flush with the body at the rear, whilst the one-piece fronts were frameless to give the car a clean look. Every time a door was opened or closed these first lowered a fraction and then closed to avoid having to slam the door. The profile was still unmistakably that of a 911, but with fewer curves and a wider and longer stance, it certainly seemed a more modern interpretation of the classic theme, and a touch more purposeful at the same time.

For the latest 911 the wheelbase was made 2350mm (92.5in) long – an increase of 78mm (3.1in)

continued page 57

The new 911 certainly made a splash wherever it went! This picture shows the rear spoiler in its erect position.

The front mask was definitely fresh, but still recognizable as a 911, especially with the headlights on.

The new 911 at rest. Detailing was exceptional on the 996 body: recessed rain gutters gave the roof a clean profile, flush door handles and integrated door mirrors added modernity. Enlarging the glasshouse and raising the bumper height gave the car a more compact appearance than its dimensions suggested. However, some testers complained that the doors didn't shut with the familiar, precise noise of earlier 911s, and the trigger-style door handles were sorely missed by diehard 911 enthusiasts. The body had a ten-year anti-perforation warranty.

53

The rear spoiler in its deployed and usual positions.

54

Dashboard of a manual car for continental Europe.

As was traditional with the 911, the instrument panel was dominated by a central tachometer, marked up to 8000rpm and with the red-line at 7200 for the 996. The speedo (calibrated up to 175mph or 300kph depending on the market) sat to its left, with a voltmeter to the far left. To the right, the temperature and fuel gauges were in one meter (which also featured gear selection on Tiptronic cars), whilst oil pressure was in a separate meter on the far right. The clock was now a digital affair, tucked in underneath the fuel gauge once the oil level indicator faded away shortly after start-up. The digital odometer and trip computer features were integrated at the bottom of the tachometer and speedometer; the bank of warning lights ran along the lower edge of the instrument pack.

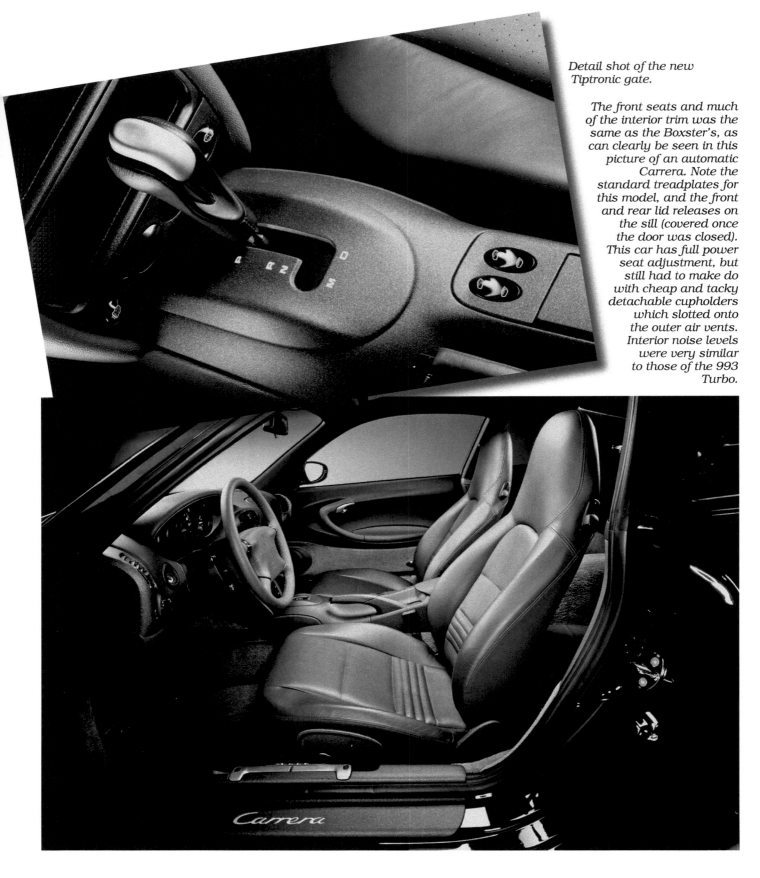

*Detail shot of the new
Tiptronic gate.*

*The front seats and much
of the interior trim was the
same as the Boxster's, as
can clearly be seen in this
picture of an automatic
Carrera. Note the
standard treadplates for
this model, and the front
and rear lid releases on
the sill (covered once
the door was closed).
This car has full power
seat adjustment, but
still had to make do
with cheap and tacky
detachable cupholders
which slotted onto
the outer air vents.
Interior noise levels
were very similar
to those of the 993
Turbo.*

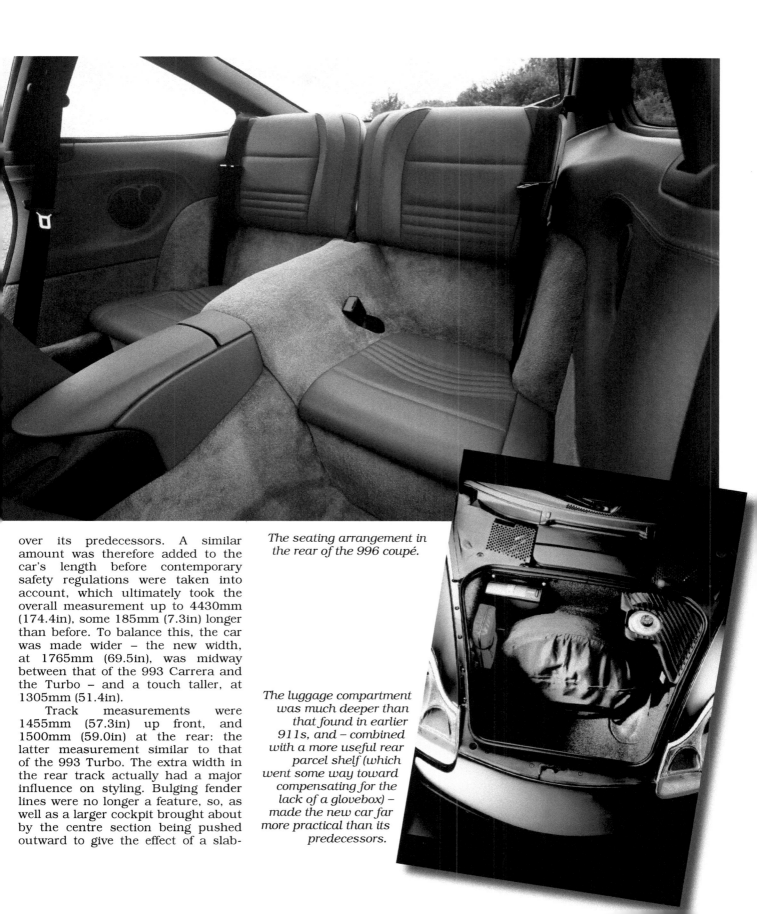

over its predecessors. A similar amount was therefore added to the car's length before contemporary safety regulations were taken into account, which ultimately took the overall measurement up to 4430mm (174.4in), some 185mm (7.3in) longer than before. To balance this, the car was made wider – the new width, at 1765mm (69.5in), was midway between that of the 993 Carrera and the Turbo – and a touch taller, at 1305mm (51.4in).

Track measurements were 1455mm (57.3in) up front, and 1500mm (59.0in) at the rear: the latter measurement similar to that of the 993 Turbo. The extra width in the rear track actually had a major influence on styling. Bulging fender lines were no longer a feature, so, as well as a larger cockpit brought about by the centre section being pushed outward to give the effect of a slab-

The seating arrangement in the rear of the 996 coupé.

The luggage compartment was much deeper than that found in earlier 911s, and – combined with a more useful rear parcel shelf (which went some way toward compensating for the lack of a glovebox) – made the new car far more practical than its predecessors.

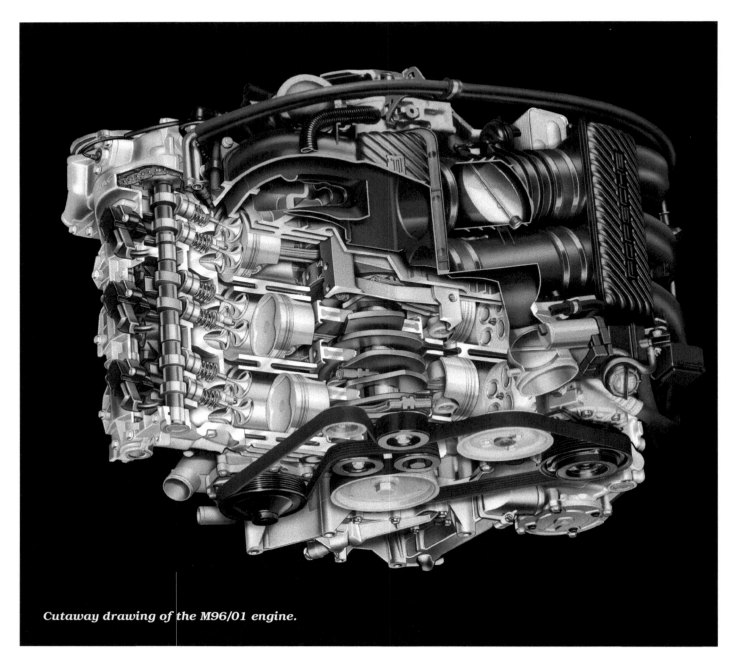

Cutaway drawing of the M96/01 engine.

sided vehicle, the tail was fatter and heavier looking.

As with other recent 911s, the rear spoiler usually sat flush on the engine cover, the 996 version raising automatically at 75mph (120kph) and dropping again once the pace decreased to half that speed; it could also be controlled manually via a switch on the dash. An interesting feature was the extra third brake light

in the trailing edge of the spoiler, as once the wing was deployed, it made it difficult to see the main one mounted close to the lower edge of the rear window.

There were plans to produce the 996 with an all-aluminium body structure, but cost limitations later ruled this out. Nonetheless, the galvanized steel body was lighter and quicker to build than before, yet

possessed significantly more torsional rigidity (said to be up to 45 per cent stiffer), and played host to a fresh interior.

The interior was basically an updated version of the traditional 911 concept, with a strong Boxster influence. In fact, there were very few differences between the two water-cooled Porsches: Minor detail changes included five gauges under an enclosed

A rather more orthodox view of the 996 power unit (note the interesting exhaust arrangement). The new 911s had a 12,000 mile (20,000km) service interval, but new technology made servicing quicker and cheaper than ever before.

hood for the 911 (reduced in size and overlapping each other to make them easier to read through the four-spoke steering wheel, now adjustable for reach); different air vents and switches on the centre console, and, of course, the addition of rear seats. As before, these were for children or occasional use only, and could be folded to give extra luggage space.

Despite the high level of standard trim and equipment, and the extra bulk, the car's weight was kept down to just 1320kg (2904lb) – 50kg (110lb) less than the 993 coupé when that model was launched. The 996 was far more crashworthy than its predecessors, too, more aerodynamic (thanks to some fine detailing, above and below the floor, with a drag co-efficient of just Cd 0.30), and lift was reduced at both ends.

Engine & transmission details
One tends to associate Porsche with air-cooled powerplants, but combining air cooling with modern technology was never an easy task. Racing engines with four valves per cylinder had to adopt water-cooled heads, which increased expense and engineering complexity, and exhaust and noise pollution regulations were becoming stricter with each passing year – one

of the main reasons Ernst Fuhrmann took Porsche down the water-cooled route with the 924 and 928. In reality, after looking at a four-litre air-cooled unit and quickly dismissing it, the men at Weissach were left with little alternative but to develop a new line of water-cooled engines for the 986 and 996 – a pair of all alloy, 24v flat-sixes, with a 2.5-litre unit specified for the Boxster, and a 3.4-litre version reserved for the new 911.

The 996 was powered by the M96/01 engine in all markets. The early 3.4-litre crankcase was very similar to that of the Boxster (it had the same bore centres to allow manufacture via the same machines, being the same as those of the last air-cooled flat-six). It was basically a two-piece aluminium alloy casting playing host to a separate carrier with seven main bearings for the forged steel crank, and a silicon lining on the cylinder walls.

With a bore and stroke of 96 x 78mm, the cubic capacity of the M96/01 lump was 3387cc. As a matter of interest, the short stroke, oversquare characteristics were carried over from the Boxster engine (Type M96/20), although a bore and stroke measurement of 85.5 x 72mm gave a 2480cc displacement for the two-seater.

Anyway, the 3.4-litre, water-cooled, 24v flat-six featured forged aluminium pistons, attached to the crankshaft by cracked forged steel conrods. Dry sump lubrication was carried over from the air-cooled days, but not in the traditional format. In the 996's case, although separated from the crank chamber, the tank was integrated into the engine design, in the same location as a regular sump. However, the benefits of a dry sump were retained, while the new arrangement saved on lengthy hoses and gave neater packaging; no fewer than three pumps were used to keep the oil moving, and the new car was also equipped with an oil/water coolant heat exchanger.

Radiators were positioned below each headlight (it took many experiments to satisfy the various technical, packaging and styling requirements) with hoses running back most of the length of the car toward the engine to feed the cross-flow water jackets. Incidentally, a third radiator was placed under the front number plate on automatic cars to cool transmission fluid.

At the top end, the heads were the same on both sides. While this saved money from a manufacturing point of view, with the camshaft drive sprocket at only one end, it was necessary to have drive chains at both the front and rear of the engine. At least the engine ancillaries were driven off a single self-adjusting ribbed belt, thus easing servicing requirements; camshaft drive chains were also self-adjusting and maintenance-free.

With a double overhead cam per bank arrangement (the intake camshafts uppermost with the exhaust camshafts lower down), hydraulic lifters for the valves, and Variocam variable valve timing, it was a very advanced powerplant. To add to the complexity, the 911 unit also had a new, albeit simplified version of the Varioram variable induction system (with fixed runners and a valve placed in the crossover pipe connecting the left and right plenum chambers), something the Boxster had to do without.

A single sparkplug was located in the centre of the combustion chamber roof, each fed by its own mini coil. The Bosch Motronic DME fuel-injection and ignition system was selected, the M5.2 version coming with hot-film air mass metering, and oxygen sensors in the exhaust. Exhaust manifolds were manufactured in stainless steel, with a catalytic converter for each bank situated aft of the engine, between the two tailpipes that exited from the rear valance – one each side of the number plate housing. Interestingly, the exhaust note was tuned to make it sound like the old air-cooled machine.

Layout drawing showing the packaging arrangements for the 996.

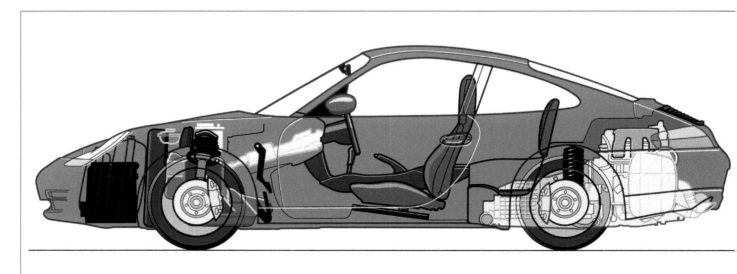

The air/fuel mix was delivered to the cylinders via a part plastic (the uppermost section containing the Varioram mechanism), part alloy intake manifold, and with an 11.3:1 compression ratio, the 996 engine gave 300bhp DIN (296bhp SAE nett) at 6800rpm on premium (high octane) unleaded, although it would run quite happily on lower grade fuels. Maximum torque was put at 258lbft at 4600rpm, but the torque curve was quite flat and very accessible thanks to Variocam, with 85 per cent of torque available from 2700rpm all the way up to 200rpm off the red line.

Despite having more camshafts and valves, the water-cooled unit actually had far fewer parts than the old air-cooled sixes, largely due to the crankcase design, which came with three cylinders already cast in, thus eliminating the need for separate barrels, as in older flat-six Porsche engines. In addition, as well as delivering more power, better economy (officially 23.9mpg on average) and lower emissions, the latest engine was still more compact than the previous 911 unit.

The new Carrera engine had the same M96/01 code, regardless of whether a manual or automatic gearbox was fitted. And that brings us nicely onto the transmission options ...

The manual transmission was still a six-speed unit, but lighter and more compact than before. Sourced from Getrag and given the Type G96/00 designation, it came with internal ratios of 3.82 on first, 2.20 on second, 1.52 on third, 1.22 on fourth, 1.02 on fifth, and 0.84 on sixth; a 3.44:1 final-drive was specified. Shift actuation was by cable rather than rod, as found on the earlier 911s. The six forward speeds were laid out in a double-H pattern in three planes, with reverse up and to the left outside this grouping. The manual gearbox employed a 240mm (9.4in) diameter clutch mounted on a dual-mass flywheel.

The Tiptronic S semi-automatic transmission was based on the old version, but the number of forward speeds was increased from four to five. The selector was marked up with Park, Reverse, Neutral and Drive, with 'M' for Manual to the left of Drive, which allowed the driver to go

Front and rear suspension, steering and braking system of the 996. Note the extensive use of aluminium alloy throughout the suspension at both ends, as well as the drilled and ventilated brake discs.

Cutaway drawing revealing all the major components which combine to form the heart and soul of the new 911.

The sprawling Weissach complex certainly proved its worth during the 996's development phase.

up and down through the ratios via the steering wheel-mounted buttons. Built by ZF, the Type A96/00 Tiptronic transmission added 45kg (99lb) to the car's kerb weight, and came with internal ratios of 3.66, 2.00, 1.41, 1.00, 0.74 and a 3.68:1 final-drive.

The 996 was available with traction control – a 40 per cent torque-controlled limited-slip differential combined with ABD (Automatic Brake Differential). This rear axle device worked with the lsd to direct power to whichever wheel had the most grip, using the ABS sensors to gather information, then applying the brakes and adjusting engine torque in varying degrees to best keep the car on its chosen path. The traction control system could be switched off for spirited driving, though.

By the way, there were rumours

of a 3-litre engine, which could have then been employed as an optional powerplant for the Boxster, but the smaller unit never made it to the marketplace. Indeed, when the Boxster acquired more powerful engines ready for the 2000 season, the base unit went from 2.5 to 2.7-litres, and the S was introduced with a 3.2-litre lump. Interestingly, Horst Marchart had not entirely ruled out a revival of the air-cooled six ...

The 996's underpinnings

Naturally, with a front end more or less shared with the Boxster, the new 911's front suspension was very similar to that of the two-seater. However, packaging considerations brought about by the different layouts (the 986 being an MR car, while the 996 had an RR configuration) led to a completely different rear suspension on the 911.

The front suspension, mounted on an alloy subframe, featured coil springs over MacPherson struts, with cast aluminium alloy lower control arms, and a 23mm (0.90in) anti-roll bar on manual machines (automatics came with a slightly thicker bar).

An independent multi-link system was used at the rear, mounted on an alloy subframe. Four of the five links on each side formed double-wishbones around the coil spring over damper unit, the latter mounted just aft of the driveshafts; the rear anti-roll bar was 18.5mm (0.73in) in diameter. Interestingly, rubber bushings were designed to make the outer front wheel toe-out slightly when cornering, and the outer rear wheel toe-in, thus endowing the car with predictable understeer on the limit.

As usual, a lowered Sport suspension package (M030) was available, including harder springs and dampers, and beefier anti-roll bars (up to 23.5mm/0.92in at the front, as used on AT cars, and 19.5mm/0.77in on the rear of manual models). The front crossmember was revised soon after production began, incidentally, along with the rear track rod.

The dual circuit brakes incorporated the Bosch version 5.3 ABS system. Front discs were shared with the Boxster (318mm/12.5in in diameter and 28mm/1.1in thick), and the front, four-pot calipers were basically the same as 986 items, too, with unequal pistons in a monobloc alloy casting. The rear discs were unique to the 996, however (299mm/11.8in in diameter and 24mm/0.9in thick, with integrated brake drums for the handbrake), although, unlike the front discs, the rears were not handed.

The power-assisted rack-and-pinion steering had a 16.9:1 ratio to give three turns lock-to-lock. The telescopic column allowed adjustable reach on the steering wheel – a first for the 911.

Regarding wheel and tyre combinations, standard fare for the 996 was a 17-inch cast-alloy, five-spoke design (M396). There was a 7J rim with 205/50 ZR-rated rubber up front, and 9J rims shod with 255/40 ZR17s at the rear.

As an option, the owner could specify an 18-inch wheel and tyre combination, with 7.5J rims up front (with 225/40 rubber), and 10Js at the rear (with 265/35s). According to several contemporary tests, the larger tyres were prone to squeal at quite low cornering speeds, but probably gave the best ride/handling compromise when combined with the regular suspension set-up. Two 18-inch designs were available initially – the multi-spoke 'Sport Classic II' (XRB) rim, and the five-spoke 'Turbo Look' (M413) wheel.

Testing, testing ...

Spy photographs of the new 911 began appearing in enthusiast publications during the late summer and autumn of 1996, although retouched pictures – very accurate ones, too, it has to be said – were appearing much earlier.

Both closed and open versions of the 996 were snapped circulating Weissach and on the track at Nardo in Italy, painted black and with light disguise panels in a vain attempt to outwit the long lens brigade. Testing also took place in the States, and in Australia, where high speed driving could be experienced in extreme heat – the Northern Territory, an area without speed limits, providing ideal conditions for Porsche engineers. Cold weather testing took place mainly in Canada.

Closer to home, the demanding curves of the old Nürburgring were the ultimate handling test, and it was no mean feat that Porsche's drivers were able to knock six seconds off the lap time recorded by the equivalent 993 model. Official figures gave the 996 a top speed of 174mph (278kph), so it was no slouch, that's for sure.

As the launch date drew closer and dealers were briefed on the new car (dealer launches took place in

Testing in America.

Cold weather testing in Canada.

The shaker-bed can add the equivalent of years of use to components in a remarkably short space of time.

The 996 making its debut at the 1997 Frankfurt Show, held from 11-21 September that year.

A 996 Carrera for the home market shod with 18-inch Turbo Look alloys.

Engine bay of an early 996 model. Note the use of two struts to automatically hold up the lid.

65

Rear view of one of the original publicity cars. The number plate will come in useful once again with the launch of the next generation of water-cooled models.

March 1997), photographs of pre-production prototypes began to appear in print, either running on Stuttgart trade plates or proper Ludwigsburg registration numbers. Unlike the Boxster, official pictures of the 996 were not released until quite close to the car's debut, but anyone even remotely interested had a pretty good idea of what to expect by the time the Frankfurt Show opened its doors to the public.

Initial press reaction

Long before the 57th IAA, where the 996 made its debut, the press was given a chance to sample the new 911 in southern Spain to enable reports to appear in the long-lead magazines at the same time as the car's official launch. More press ride-and-drive events were held in St Tropez, as soon as the Frankfurt event opened to the public.

There were worries, of course, that the loss of the air-cooled engine would rob this most famous of motoring icons of its spirit. Mac DeMere of *Motor Trend* fame declared: "Though the 996 intentionally carries the essence of every 911 before it – from the 1963 901 on – and shares development costs and many components with the Boxster, the 1999 911 is a true, clean sheet, from the ground up, new design. But is this new creation so new that it's no longer a true 911? No way. The 996 feels, sounds, and drives so much like the previous edition that some will falsely suspect it's another remake of the original."

Writing for *Autocar*, Peter Robinson noted: "It's a marvellous engine, incredibly smooth and more refined than the old, yet still sporting, always invigorating, and alive with stronger mid-range power than the Boxster; there's not the same need to keep the crank spinning above 4000rpm. In fact, the Carrera pulls from as low as 2000rpm and never lets up, delivering a mighty, linear urge until it hits the soft electronic limiter at 7300rpm."

In another *Autocar* article, it was stated: "Unsurprisingly, considering there's not a turbocharger in sight, and that it uses a close-ratio six-speed gearbox in which even top stretches only 25.7mph out of every 1000rpm, throttle response is as sharp as it is wonderful in the new car. And as with all previous 911s, flexibility is towering."

The gearchange quality in the lower ratios was criticized in *Motor Sport*, although being a test car, abuse from earlier drives sprang to mind as the reason for this. However, stopping power was never in question, and easily up to the car's performance. Csaba Csere reported in *Car & Driver* that: "As on previous 911 variants, these brakes feel powerful, consistent, and immensely reassuring."

Visibility was said to be excellent for a car of this type (although the A-pillars were broader than on earlier 911s), the Boxster seats were good (as an option, bucket seats had been available on the 911 since 1989 through the Exclusive programme), and there was greater leg-, shoulder- and headroom than before. Heating and ventilation was much better due to the water-cooled engine providing a more consistent stream of heat, and ergonomics were vastly improved, although one tester remarked that the "beautifully made cabin just doesn't feel as tough as that of the old car."

The driving position was said to be just about perfect, with the all-new pendant-style pedals no longer being offset (a proper footrest sat to the left of the pedal set), and, at last, the steering wheel was adjustable, albeit for reach only. However, while not an issue in the majority of road tests, compared to earlier 911s, some steering feel was lost according to a number of contemporary articles. On the other hand, combined with superior ride quality and insulation from road noise, the car was less tiring to drive, thanks to this slight dulling of wheel reaction, and gave the impression of greater straight-line stability.

The car's unruffled refinement often gave the driver the impression he was travelling far slower than the speedo reading. But on twisty stretches, the 911 had lost very little of its character. As *Autocar* observed: "Sensational grip and virtually unlimited traction are matched by steering that's close to perfect in its meaty feel, the way it weights up a touch as lateral forces rise and the agility of its turn-in, yet it isn't so sensitive that it demands constant concentration at Autobahn speeds. There's no more than a hint of the traditional 911 jiggle, while the tighter turning circle brings immediate benefits in creating a perception of nimble responsiveness, despite the extra width and length.

"Working with wheel and throttle, you can place the Carrera exactly as you like. The handling and steering responses are more progressive, perfectly linear. You can hold the car in a neutral stance, feeding in enough power to delicately change its attitude inch by inch, if that is what's required to clip an apex. On the other hand, drop down a gear or two through the decisive yet fluid gearchange and it's easy to power out of a corner in a mild, predictable oversteer slide that demands no more than a rolling of the wrists. Yes, it's more fun than the old car, more satisfying and more consistent in its behaviour, despite the 61% rear weight bias. It's still a true sports car."

Road & Track's Joe Rusz added: "According to Lagaay, even the most conservative Porsche customers and dealers wound up embracing the new 911 within minutes after being exposed to it at a design clinic. Had they driven it, as I did, they would have discovered that the latest Carrera is quieter, more rigid, roomier and more comfortable, plus faster and more stable than the current model ... On balance, this is the best 911 yet."

The home market

While the 996 Carrera was making its debut in Germany in September, the 993 series soldiered on into the 1998 model year, as the 996 was available in rear-wheel drive coupé form only initially.

The 1997 Frankfurt Show ran from 11-21 September. At this time, the Boxster (by now built at the Valmet Automotive plant in Uusikaupunki, Finland, as well as Zuffenhausen) provided entry-level Porsche motoring for DM 76,500, while at DM 135,650, the new 996 Carrera was the cheapest of the 911s. Of the 993 models, the

Targa was listed at DM 146,500, and the Carrera 4 was DM 143,500 in regular guise, or DM 159,800 in C4S spec; the Turbo commanded a hefty DM 222,500.

Within weeks of the launch, a body kit had become available for the new Carrera – the so-called 'Cup' Aero Kit (code XAA) being the first to appear. This included a rather attractive apron for the front airdam, side skirts (complete with matching pieces on the rear valance), and a fixed rear spoiler similar to that found on the 996-based Supercup racers.

Other options included the 18-inch alloys described earlier; coloured emblems for the wheel centres (instead of the regular black); colour-keyed wheels and special paint for the coachwork; the Sport chassis modifications (with or without traction control); a sunroof; headlight washers; a rear wiper; a roof rack; a parking assistance system; a combination package including stainless steel exhaust trims (X54), steel treadplates and white-faced instruments (all available separately); normal or gathered leather trim (along with the option of custom colours); full power adjustment and lumbar support for the front seats; embossed headrests; cloth

Evolution 911

PORSCHE

Advertising that says it all ...

seat inlays; heated seats; Sport seats (with the added option of a painted seatback); interior trim packages (including carbon accents, or light or dark maple burr); gearknob and handbrake trim in aluminium/leather, aluminium/carbon, and aluminium/ maple burr combinations; a three-spoke leather-wrapped steering wheel; steering wheels with carbon and leather trim, maple and leather, or all leather (including the centre pad); an onboard computer; the chance to exchange the ashtray and cigarette lighter for a storage compartment; a ten-speaker audio system, which could then be upgraded via a digital

sound package, a radio/CD unit or CD autochanger; an active carbon air filtration system; carpeting, stitching and other trim items in a different colour to standard; floormats; footwell lighting; carbon treadplates; seatbelts in red, yellow or blue rather than the regular black; the deletion of external badging, and PCM.

The Porsche Communication Management system (PCM) used a large screen in the centre console to play host to the navigation system, stereo, onboard computer, and hands-free carphone. It should be noted that the heater controls in cars fitted with PCM were moved to a new position,

lower down in the centre console, where access was often hampered by the gearstick.

The new car in America
In America, Frederick Schwab was still President of PCNA, but the company now worked out of a new address in Atlanta, Georgia. The move occurred in March 1998, allowing the US head office to be closer to Porsche's POE at Charleston, South Carolina. It also opened up the opportunity to build a manufacturing plant in the States; an ideal way to overcome exchange rate fluctuations, although ultimately nothing happened in this direction.

The late Paul Frère – doyen of motoring writers, highly successful racing driver, and arch 911 enthusiast – with the 1998 Ruf CTR. The 993-based model was one of the fastest cars in the world.

The early 1999 model year 996 coupé was announced in January 1998, although sales didn't begin until the spring to coincide with the official launch of the Cabriolet. Fans and potential clients had the chance to see both 996 variants at the Detroit Show, where the new 911 made its US debut.

Engine and transmission options were the same as those offered elsewhere in the world, with the 3.4-litre six attached to either a manual six-speed or semi-automatic five-speed gearbox. The EPA rated the new 911 at 17/25 in MT guise, and 16/25 in AT form.

Standard equipment on the coupé included foglights, air conditioning, a power sunroof, partial electric adjustment on the front seats, remote central locking, cruise control, power windows with tinted glass, heated power door mirrors, a four-speaker radio/cassette, an alarm system, part-leather upholstery, and a leather-wrapped steering wheel. Incidentally, side airbags were also standard in the US (optional in other markets).

Road & Track's Kim Reynolds was not impressed by the 996 at the press launch, as he openly admitted. His image of the old 911 was too strong, so he travelled to the Nürburgring with Paul Frère to put the 993 and 996 through a back-to-back test. He noted: "I fire up my old love, the air-cooled 911, and am instantly struck with how dramatic the 996's technical advance really is. The older car rides more nervously; braking into a corner, I subconsciously become a coiled spring ready to deploy a counter-steering jerk of the steering wheel if the rear wheels even sneeze

Indeed, Porsche's links with Valmet grew stronger instead.

However, Porsche's presence in the US was strengthened by the establishment of Porsche Engineering Services in Detroit in 1991, which originally did little more than liaise with American customers and Weissach, but in more recent years has become a recognized specialist in body engineering, even helping to refine construction techniques used on the Boxster and 996.

Meanwhile, with a few 993s still being sold, the air-cooled machines were classed as 1998 vehicles, while the new 996 was promoted as a ridiculously early 1999 model. For 1998, the base rear-wheel drive 993-type Carrera coupé was dropped, along with the 911 Turbo S. Until stocks ran out, this left the Carrera S at $63,750, the C4S at $73,000, the Targa at $70,750, the Cabriolet at $73,000, and the C4 Cabriolet at $78,350; the Turbo was officially discontinued for 1998, but a few remained in stock at the start of the season, listed at $105,000.

sideways. The shifter is very good – but it's not as slick as the shorter-throw 996's.

"Months earlier, during my lunchtime debate over the merits of the new 911, I had condemned it. Now I'm not so sure. You can't finish a fast lap in these two cars at a place like this and not conclude that the new Porsche is a significantly faster and, well, yes, a better car. Raced side by side, the 996 would humble the older car. And driven home, it would be quieter and more comfortable, and carry more luggage."

The article noted that axle tramp had been virtually eliminated, that lifting off the throttle in a corner was no longer a cardinal sin, and that braking was exceptional (over 1.0g being recorded at times). The new car also posted some pretty impressive performance figures – 4.6 seconds for the 0-60 dash, and a 13.2 second standing-quarter.

However, Reynolds was still "not a wholesale convert. In the name of aerodynamics, the new 911 has traded away some of its looks. To reduce production costs, there are design simplifications (the frameless side windows, the less complicated door latches) that, one by one, drain off small dollops of charm."

Car & Driver compared the Carrera coupé with the latest Corvette, and while the Porsche came second, "the 911 is almost certainly the better car of the two in absolute terms." What tipped the balance in favour of the V8-engined Chevrolet (which won with 94 points to the Carrera's 92) was the value for money factor – the American car being almost $30,000 cheaper than its German rival. And, let's face it, $30,000 would buy an extremely nice second car!

In the summer, *Road & Track* pitted the new 911 Carrera against the Honda/Acura NSX, the Ferrari F355, BMW M Roadster, Dodge Viper GTS and Chevy Corvette convertible to find the best all-round sports car. The Ferrari and Porsche tied for first place at the end of the battle, with the NSX close behind in third.

Motor Trend brought together a similar group of cars, but replaced the Honda with a Lotus Esprit V8 Turbo, and added a Panoz Roadster and Aston Martin DB7 for spice.

Regarding the 911's handling, it was noted: "On the track, the functional benefits of sending the 911 to finishing school yielded a revised suspension that virtually eliminates the car's notorious end-swapping tendencies. It consistently produced lap times that could be bettered only by lightly disguised race-cars. Not unusual for a Porsche, but the new Carrera can do so without Hans Stuck manning the helm. And believe it or not, this is a totally comfortable daily driver."

Taking into account enthusiast categories like power, refinement, handling feel, comfort, styling, noise, exclusivity and fun factors, the Ferrari came out a clear winner, with the Porsche second, and the Aston and Chevrolet close behind.

Car & Driver then tried automatic versions of the 911 and lightning quick F355. The verdict went to Ferrari's F1 system, although it should be remembered that the Modena flyer was literally twice the price of the Carrera.

On the subject of speed, *Road & Track* carried out its annual survey to find the world's fastest car. The Ruf CTR2 was timed at 201.5mph (322.4kph), although the McLaren F1 was fastest, at 217.7mph (348.3mph).

A new drophead

It was around this time that Helmut Kohl lost the German elections to Gerhard Schroeder, but, in any case, workers in Zuffenhausen were probably far more interested in public reaction to their latest creation – the new 911 Cabriolet – and the fact that the last air-cooled 911 was built on 31 March 1998. The Cabriolet had been launched in Europe earlier that month at the 1998 Geneva Show (held from 5-15 March), introduced on the home market with a DM 155,160 sticker price.

An advantage of developing the 986 and 996 together was that the front end was already structurally prepared for an open car application. Only the floorpan and the body aft of the doors needed new panelwork, partly for styling reasons, partly for the additional reinforcement necessary to give the convertible its required rigidity. Even then, a number of parts (such as the rear bumper, lights, engine cover and spoiler) were carried over from the coupé.

While nowhere near as rigid as the latest coupé, at least the new Cabriolet body was significantly stronger than that of the old drophead (around 37 per cent better in torsional rigidity, and about 23 per cent stiffer in bending rigidity, in fact), and easily became the new benchmark in its class in this respect. Reports noted not a hint of scuttle shake or unwanted body movement, even on rough road surfaces.

The roof was designed and built by Car Top Systems, a company jointly owned by Porsche and Mercedes-Benz in order to share convertible roof technology. For the Carrera, CTS came up with something quite spectacular – what can best be described as a remote controlled and slightly longer version of the Boxster hood, complete with integrated tonneau cover that left the hood partially exposed, as on the two-seater.

Providing the handbrake was applied, having the top fully closed to fully open took three motors just 20 seconds to execute and absolutely no effort whatsoever on the part of the owner – there weren't even any catches to undo on the header rail. Of course, the remote control was an option (the process was usually initiated via a console switch or the door lock), but for the man with everything – or those into gadgets – it was the ultimate pose.

An attractive aluminium hardtop was included in the price, but with the three-layer soft-top being so snug, its only tangible advantage was a heated rear window (the cloth hood had a plastic rear screen). A lot of work had gone into getting the folding top right, with a magnesium alloy frame to save weight, and hood reinforcement via lightweight panels inserted between the inner and outer linings to stop it bulging at high speed. Hood up, the car displayed the same Cd 0.30 as the coupé, and a similar level of wind noise.

Four side windows gave better rear visibility, and all were power operated. The only real disappointment was that the rear seats were rather too upright for anything but the shortest trip, and the windblocker was certainly a worthwhile option, as buffeting in the cockpit was quite strong without it. There was also a clever roof rack option, which, like the Boxster rack,

The Porsche stand at the 1998 Geneva Show.

continued to allow full use of the soft-top (or hardtop) whilst in place.

The Cabriolet was introduced as an early 1999 model in all markets. Porsche claimed it was the safest convertible in the world. As well as four three-point seatbelts, dual front airbags (standard for all markets on all cars) and the option of side airbags if not already included in the package, the drophead came with a rather novel rollover bar set-up. When the onboard sensors felt there was a risk of the car overturning, two spring-loaded bars shot out from underneath covers behind the rear seats, combining with the front headrests to give passengers precious survival space. It was a neat idea, even if it did angle the rear seats uncomfortably forward.

The Cabriolet weighed 75kg (165lb) more than the coupé, but performance was much the same in the real world

– a stopwatch was needed to separate the two cars. Colour and trim options were the same as those offered on the closed car, with the hood coming in a choice of four shades: Black, Graphite Grey, Space Grey, and Metropol Blue. These were different to the 993-based Cabriolet hood colours, although Black was obviously the same, Graphite Grey was similar to Classic Grey, and Metropol Blue was not much different to the old Dark Blue; the biggest change was that Space Grey replaced Chestnut Brown.

As Peter Robinson noted at the time of the car's launch: "What the cabrio brings is more sound, an intoxicating mix of induction and exhaust, two distinct layers of music that will appeal to those who find the new coupé a little too civilized."

Georg Kacher tried a new Cabriolet for the UK's *Car*, and found:

"Oversteer is still alive and kicking, even if it now happens at a higher level of speed and g-force. Switch off the traction control and light up those fat rear tyres. Learn to modulate the loud pedal within the breakaway range. Co-ordinate the movements of your right foot with the movements of your arms. Step by step, corner by corner, you find the slide zone is actually wider than you thought, and quite accessible, too. Together, the more benign chassis, the more forgiving steering and the more responsive engine provide the tools to perform one creamy drift after another. But remember, the point of no return arrives without much warning."

Kacher summed up his article by saying: "In this car, what really matters is the raw pleasure of speed and poise, grip and noise, the thrill of force-fed fresh air. In this car, it's

From this angle, it was all too easy to mistake the new Carrera Cabriolet for a Boxster: a misconception that had the marketing people scratching their heads in the months following the launch of the latest 911 model.

the going, not the getting there, that counts."

Regarding the styling, *Top Gear's* Angus Frazer noted: "From the rear and side, the new two-wheel drive 911 Cabriolet is a much more handsome and elegant looking car than its predecessor. Its side profile is almost more speedster than cabriolet, and although its rump sits high and fat, it still looks just as aggressive. The argument continues to rage over the

continued page 77

Rear view of the same car with its beautifully crafted hardtop close at hand. The hardtop was a no cost option in most markets, and came with its own stand.

Interior of an automatic Cabriolet with a rather unique trim colour (virtually any shade was available through the Exclusive programme), and PCM. Regular audio units included the CR-11 (M320), CR-21 (M326) and CR-31 (M330) radios, and the CDR-21 (M686) radio/CD player, which could be linked up to the CDC-3 autochanger (M692). These were soon superceded by the CR-22 and CDR-32 units (M321 and M695 respectively). The power window switch moved from its traditional spot on the door to a new location on the centre console.

The Cabriolet was said to be the safest open car on the market: here's why! Combine these rollover hoops with leading edge airbag technology and a strong windscreen frame up front, and it's obvious why Porsche was confident about making such a claim.

The optional windblocker. This relatively simple device, introduced by Mazda, made an enormous difference to controlling backdraft.

The new Cabriolet looked equally stunning with the hood up or down, or with the hardtop in place. Note the location of the third brake light.

The Cabriolet was introduced at $74,460 in the US – $9430 more than the coupé – with Tiptronic adding $3420 to both models. With regard to the new drophead, Road & Track noted whilst "... driving through twisty mountain roads, the Cabriolet never showed any hint of shakes or rattles, and the extra 165lb for the convertible is not at all noticeable. With the top up, the Cabriolet's sound measurements are quite close to the coupé's, and top down with the windblocker attached, the cabin is relatively quiet."

Catalogue photograph showing the hood mechanism in operation.

Overhead shot of the new Cabriolet, giving a clear view of the interior.

new car's front. I'd go for the old car's styling every time. The new 911's headlamps just don't look right to my eyes."

While the styling was always going to be controversial – some loved it, others hated it – Frazer was quick to praise the car's refined character, and few doubted its dynamics. Even in Germany, the 911 Cabriolet won an *Auto Motor und Sport* shoot-out between the new Porsche, Benz SL 500, Chevrolet Corvette drophead and Jaguar XKR Cabriolet.

But the final words should go to Paul Frere, who, following his first run in the Cabriolet, stated in *Road & Track*: "The more I drive the 996, the

more I like it. Forget where the engine is located; this Porsche is in the world's very top class for handling. Also, the new gearbox is a gem, and that the engine can be revved 500rpm or so higher than that of the 993 makes a big difference in usable performance."

The rhd markets
The 1997 Earls Court Show ran from 16-26 October. Porsche displayed an array of 993-based 911s, the mid-engined Boxster, and the new 996 coupé. Regarding the latter, *Autocar* noted in its show preview: "It might be water-cooled, but the rest of the 911 magic is all there." Porsche fans obviously thought so, too, as there was

already an eighteen-month waiting list for the new car, long before the London event kicked off.

In the UK, the line-up remained the same as the 1997 range until February 1998, when only the C4 coupé (£64,450), C4S (£76,450), Targa (£65,950), 3.6-litre Turbo (£97,950) and GT1 were listed from the 993 series. The new 911 Carrera was announced at £64,800 (or £68,100 with Tiptronic), almost twice the price of the Boxster, available from £33,950. By the start of March 1998, only the new coupé, Boxster and GT1 were listed by PCGB, with the 996 Cabriolet coming on line a couple of months later.

Following its first full road test of the 996 coupé, *Autocar* observed: "Although it lacks decent rear seat space, the 911 is more grand tourer than sports car now. And that can be regarded in two distinctly different ways – as a positive step forward that will stand the model in fine stead come the next century, or as a crying shame that one of the most characterful and evocative cars of our time has all but disappeared. In reality, of course, it is both."

MotorSport's Andrew Frankel felt much the same. He said: "I, for one, will miss desperately the old 911. It seems ridiculous even to suggest there has ever been a better sports car. But I think it a mistake to make it the dead albatross around the neck of this new car. Forget the 911. It is gone. The new car may not be a true 911, but it is a fine car and a great Porsche. Ultimately, it is that which matters most."

When it arrived in UK showrooms in May, the Cabriolet cost £6650 more than the coupé, priced at £71,450, with Tiptronic transmission adding £3300, as usual.

Autocar compared the 996 Cabriolet with an excellent rival – the Jaguar XKR Convertible, which was a similar price, and, despite being heavier, had an almost identical power-to-weight ratio. It was found that the Stuttgart car was the more sporting of the two, while the Coventry machine was far superior if classed as a GT. In summation the article stated: "The Porsche 911 is unique. As hard to pigeon-hole as ever, it's still the special character it always was. And of this pair, the superior driver's car."

Japan began the 1998 model year as the 1997 season had ended, selling the 993 cars until stocks ran dry, although distribution was duly taken in-house (as had happened in other parts of Europe at the time) with the formation of Porsche Japan. Having been announced at the 1997 Tokyo Show, the 996 went on sale in the Land of the Rising Sun in January 1998. The standard manual coupé

911 Cabriolets old and new.

Half a century of progress; the new Cabriolet with Porsche Number One.

was priced at 9,900,000 yen – about the same as the Mercedes-Benz SL320 – with Tiptronic transmission adding 800,000 yen. The so-called Comfort package was 145,000 yen extra, while the Sport package was available at 165,000 yen.

Paul Frere tried the 996 coupé for *Car Graphic*, and summed it up with the following words: "The new 911 is definitely faster and much more comfortable – a wonderful car. But as for being more fun, well, that's a different matter ..."

Interestingly, Frere recommended

the larger 18-inch wheels and tyres combined with the standard suspension as the best set-up for normal road use, as the Sport suspension was more suited to club racing.

Australians were expecting to have the 996 in the showrooms by mid-1998, although it was actually listed from April, alongside the last of the 993s. The 996 Carrera coupé was introduced at $183,900, while the 993 Carrera S coupé commanded $192,900, the 993 Targa was $196,900 ($11,000 less

than the Carrera Cabriolet), the 993 C4S $219,900, and the 993 Turbo $299,900. Everything then stayed the same until the end of the 1998 model year in Australia, when the entire range became 996-based.

The 1998 racing season
Porsche really didn't have to hurry with a new GT1 or GT2 weapon, as the GT1 was homologated until 2004, and both the Carrera RS 3.8 and Turbo GT2 were cleared for racing by the FIA through to the same year. But, Porsche being Porsche, there was little

A couple of shots taken by the author at the 1997 Tokyo Show, when the new Carrera made its debut in Japan. This car has the optional 18-inch Turbo Look wheels.

ミツワとポルシェ

number of detail engine modifications, such as twin ignition and more precise boost control. The air-cooled unit produced 485bhp at 5750rpm, and 490lbft of torque at 5000rpm. A hefty DM 506,000 was the asking price for the 1100kg (2420lb) racer, with DM 287,500 quoted for those brave enough to opt for the proposed road legal, 450bhp version. With the 996-based Turbo some way off, Porsche had little choice but to continue developing the 993 GT2.

To complete the picture, in October 1997 (only a couple of weeks after the 996 launch), the first competition version of the water-cooled 911 range was introduced – the six-speed 911 GT3 Cup. The strengthened and lightened body (door skins and the rear lid/spoiler were made in

Striking cover from the December 1997 issue of Car Graphic. From this angle, the new Carrera appears far more curvaceous than when viewed directly from the front or side.

chance of the company resting on its laurels.

Announced at the Porsche Cup prize-giving at the end of November 1997, the GT1/98 was the Zuffenhausen concern's answer to the Mercedes-Benz CLK-GTR. It had a full carbonfibre body, and weighed in at just 940kg (2068lb). Spawned under the leadership of Norbert Singer, the new car, homologated on 1 April 1998 and duly allocated the homologation number GT1-09, was lighter, stiffer, longer, lower and wider than its predecessor.

The GT2 category also had a new contender. The 1998 GT2 Evolution had less weight, a new front spoiler and a taller rear spoiler, improved brakes and suspension, plus a

Another Japanese advert from the time, issued by Porsche Japan and showing the new Carrera Cabriolet. Incidentally, standard anti-roll bar diameters for this model were 23.5mm (0.92in) up front, and 18.5mm (0.73in) at the rear.

the points of its Stuttgart neighbour, which finished second. Porsche drivers Yannick Dalmas and Allan McNish shared fifth spot in the drivers' table, and even the GT2 category failed to provide the desired silverware.

For one year only, the GTR Euroseries was launched by former BPR man, Stephane Ratel, to give privateers a chance to race on a lower budget than that demanded by the FIA GT Championship. Of the five rounds, Porsche drivers won four, but the trophy was ultimately hoisted aloft by a McLaren pilot.

The IMSA series was in the wilderness, taking on the Professional Sports Car Racing (PSCR) moniker, but little would happen in America until the American Le Mans Series (ALMS) was formed in 1999, thanks to the initiative of Don Panoz. Meanwhile, although Porsche drivers couldn't make a clean sweep as they had in 1997, at least GT2 fell to the Stuttgart marque, with Larry Schumacher winning the category convincingly.

The SCCA USRRC, which became Can-Am in the 1960s, was resurrected in 1998, with the 24 hours of Daytona kicking things off. A Porsche GT1 came second overall (first in Class), driven by Allan McNish, Danny Sullivan, Dirk Muller, Uwe Alzen and Jorg Muller, and GT2 also fell to the Stuttgart maker, with Franz Konrad's

continued page 89

plastics to save weight) played host to a 3.6-litre M96/75 engine, rated at 360bhp at 7200rpm, and numbered from 63W20001 onwards. The first cars (chassis 698001-698029) were used in the Supercup series, won in 1998 by reigning champion Patrick Huisman, who then went on to retain the title in 1999 and 2000.

In the FIA GT Championship, Mercedes-Benz managed to dominate the season, winning all ten rounds and finishing on nearly three times

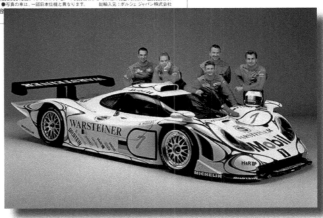

Class of '98. From left to right, we can see Jorg Muller, Uwe Alzen, Bob Wollek, Allan McNish and Yannick Dalmas pictured with the GT1/98.

Porsche fulfilled its promise to build a GT1 road car, and began producing a planned 30 units in the spring of 1997 under Chief Project Engineer Gerhard Heid and Hartmut Kristen. However, the body lines of these DM 1,550,000 vehicles were quite different to those of the original car, taking into account the styling of the 996s. This is the 544bhp street version of the GT1/98, which tipped the scales at just 1150kg (2530lb), pictured in March 1998. The racing version was known as the GT1 Evolution.

The 1998 Supercup racer at the time of its announcement. Note the 18-inch BBS alloys, and the front and rear spoilers, augmented by side skirts on the sills. The rear spoiler was available as an option for the regular Carrera; eventually, a road version of the GT3 made its way into the showrooms.

Action from Le Mans, June 1998. This was Porsche's 16th victory at the famous French circuit.

GT3 Cup cars being built up in the Porsche competition shop. The rollcage was installed by an outside contractor, but everything else was done in-house.

Tennis legend Henri Leconte donning a helmet in the Supercup.

GT2 coming in fourth overall. Porsche ultimately won the GT1 and GT2 titles at the end of the year, and came second in GT3; Thierry Boutsen won the GT1 driver's laurels with a 911 GT1.

In the 1998 Japanese Grand Touring Championship (JGTC), there were a couple of GT500 runners (the top category), plus quite a few 911s in GT300. Homegrown winners came through in both Classes, however. Paul Frere rightly once said that the 996 would never be considered a true 911 until it was victorious in racing. Its time would come ...

At least there was success in the Le Mans 24-hour Race, where the GT1/98 of Allan McNish, Laurent Aiello and Stephane Ortelli crossed the line first, one lap ahead of a sister car driven by Jorg Muller, Uwe Alzen and Bob Wollek, and four laps ahead of Nissan's dream team. GT2 went to a Chrysler Viper GTS-R, but it's the car that takes the flag first that people remember. Singer's efforts were rewarded, and Porsche secured its 16th outright victory at the Sarthe circuit.

Shot from the Hockenheim round of the Supercup, clearly showing the new water-cooled engine.

It's nice to celebrate a 50th anniversary among friends.

Porsche 911 GT1: first and second at the 1998 24 Hours of Le Mans.

Porsche. Since 1948, there is no substitute.

PORSCHE

Advertising produced to commemorate Porsche's 1998 win at Le Mans. Incidentally, the famous Porsche emblem was revised slightly from the start of the 993 series, and continued unchanged for the 996. It gained black script at the top of the badge, and the centre was simplified, as well as slightly reduced in size. As a whole, the badge was fractionally wider than before, although calipers would be required to appreciate the difference.

Magnificent car in a magnificent setting – a fitting tailpiece for this chapter ...

The death of Ferry Porsche

Born in Wiener-Neustadt (just south of Vienna) in Austria on 19 September 1909, Ferdinand Anton Ernst Porsche, better known as Ferry, was the son of Professor Ferdinand Porsche, creator of the legendary Auto Union racers and the Volkswagen Beetle.

Ferry had worked alongside his famous father on many projects before and during the war, but it was after the conflict that he began to shine in his own right. First, he designed and built the Cisitalia (a flat-12 Grand Prix car), and then turned his attention to building a sports car based on VW components. The was the Type 356 – the first vehicle to actually bear the Porsche family name, and the foundation stone for the company that we all know and love today.

Ferry's leadership skills were as finely honed as his engineering acumen, and the car-making business (which started in Gmünd in Austria) was soon expanding at its new site in Stuttgart. Ferry had racing in his blood, and Porsches were seen in all manner of competition before the 550 Spyder put the marque on the map. More racers followed, and the 356 was developed through lessons learnt at the race track.

The 911, designed by Ferry's son, Butzi, became Porsche's most famous model. His nephew, Ferdinand Piech, was also involved with the project, and in more recent years became head of the Volkswagen group – now a vast business empire, but originally built on the designs of Ferry's father in the 1930s.

The 911 duly achieved greatness, and Porsche's exploits in motorsport took on legendary status, just as the Silver Arrows had before WWII. The introduction of water-cooled engines and a new line of vehicles threatened to prematurely kill off Ferry's favourite model, but the 911 survived thanks to his faith in the rear-engined car.

Ferry Porsche kept a tight grip on the helm in Stuttgart, even in his 80s, helping to guide the company through a series of ups and downs. The great man passed away on 27

Ferry Porsche pictured with the 30th anniversary 911 in 1993.

March 1998 leaving behind four sons: Ferdinand Alexander (Butzi), Gerhard Anton (Gerd), Hans Peter (usually addressed simply as Peter), and Wolfgang Heinz (Wolfi).

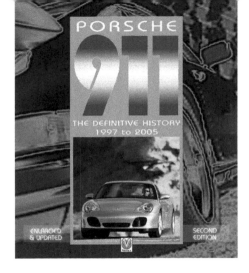

4

Establishing the water-cooled cars

The 1999 season was an important one in Porsche history, as the entire mainstream line-up was powered by water-cooled engines – the first time this had happened since the Stuttgart marque's foundation.

Although both the coupé and the drophead versions of the new 911 were classed as early 1999 models, the 1999 season proper (from September 1998) saw the introduction of a new Carrera 4 variant. Like many other contemporary magazines, *Autocar* was quick to praise the latest C4, stating it "really is the nicest 996 yet."

Of course, a new season always brought with it a whole host of detail changes, especially just after a new line had been introduced. The most

Clear indicator lenses (or slightly smoked to be completely accurate) were adopted on all 1999 model 911s; the Boxster continued with orange items to give the two cars a stronger distinguishing feature at the front end. This is the strict Carrera Cabriolet for the 1999 season.

Front and (overleaf) rear views of the new Carrera 4 coupé. Note the bright badging, and the parking assistance sensors at the back of the car.

obvious of these was the adoption of clear front and rear indicator lenses on all 1999 model 911s to further distance the RR car from its mid-engined cousin.

On the mechanical side, the crank carrier design was revised, along with the camshaft chain tensioner and intermediate shaft on the cam drive (used to transmit power to the rear-driven camshaft); there were also new exhaust valves, and a modified oil pump housing and water pump. Several hoses on the cooling system were changed, and the central air duct that feeds the water-cooling radiators was modified at the front. Home market cars received revised catalytic converters, and the main muffler design was updated

on all cars. Finally, not only was the Tiptronic ECU changed – and revised virtually every year thereafter – but automatic cars also gained a new 3.55:1 final-drive.

With regard to the chassis, the rear wheel carrier was revised midway through the season, as was the rear anti-roll bar. The C4 front anti-roll bar was unique, by the way, and another was introduced for the C4 with the M030 suspension upgrade. At the rear, an 18.5mm (0.73in) bar was employed on the C4 Cabriolet (MT and AT); a 19.5mm (0.77in) bar was specified for the C4 coupé (MT and AT) and the C4 Cabriolet with the M030 option (MT and AT), while C4 coupés with the M030 suspension (MT and AT) had a 20.5mm (0.81in) item.

As before, a pre-charging hydraulic pump was used instead of a regular servo for the C4 braking system, combined with the latest ABS main hydraulic control unit

(actually, the latter was continually updated, although it remained classed as version 5.7). Most of these subtle refinements were overlooked at the time, as the introduction of the Carrera 4 simply stole everyone's attention ...

The 996 Carrera 4

The latest Carrera 4 was approved for production in February 1994, with Thomas Herold in charge of the project. Although it looked the same from the outside, the entire front structure was unique to the C4. The front suspension was moved slightly to clear the driveshafts, there was a new, slightly smaller 64-litre (14.1 imperial gallon) fuel tank, and the space-saver spare was relocated, sitting flat in the luggage compartment (now said to have a 100-litre capacity instead of the 130 listed for the strict Carrera), and inflated by a small compressor when needed.

93

A new feature for the 996 Carrera 4 was the option of Tiptronic S transmission – earlier C4s had been offered with a manual gearbox only. The automatic option became possible because the viscous coupling was moved to the front differential from the nose of the transaxle, allowing either transmission to be linked to the four-wheel-drive system. Another advantage was the shift in weight distribution, quoted as a more favourable 40 per cent front, 60 per cent rear on the C4.

Apart from relocation of the viscous clutch, the 4WD set-up was basically similar to that of the 993. Drive to the front wheels varied between 5 and 40 per cent depending on conditions, transferred by a lighter, more conventional shaft arrangement than earlier C4s, with rubber couplings at each end and a centre support for greater drivetrain refinement. The old transaxle tube was thus deleted, saving about 4kg (9lb).

Also new was the Porsche Stability Management (PSM) system. The Bosch-built PSM system worked in conjunction with the new E-gas electronic throttle, and the ABS and ABD control units. With the help of wheel speed, steering angle, lateral acceleration and yaw sensors, the system was able to perfectly calculate drift angles and step in just before a driver was liable to run into trouble. In oversteer situations, PSM brakes the outer front wheel, whilst understeer brakes the inner rear wheel, safely bringing the car back into line. It could be switched off, automatically reactivating if the brakes were applied during an overzealous slide, but the real beauty of PSM was that it was so discreet.

As *Autocar* noted: "All the driver understands is that the nose is less prone to pushing wide. The engine management system is set up so that if you lift off suddenly in a bend, a degree of torque is maintained to smooth out the weight transfer and reduce the car's reactions. It all makes for a supercar that is as failsafe as any, yet remains fun to drive quickly, the electronics doing their job so unobtrusively that most drivers won't even notice, unless they attack corners with arms flailing. Even then,

it's effectively impossible to throw the C4 off balance, at least on dry roads, though not even the C4 can defy the laws of physics.

"It takes no more than a couple of corners to fall in love with the C4. It's the normal 911, only better. More stable, especially at the high speeds the Carrera so quickly attains, less nervous in strong crosswinds, and even more consistent in its dynamics … The choice between C2 and C4 remains as complex as ever."

The C4 was powered by the M96/02 unit, basically the same as the M96/01 except for the fly-by-wire throttle (described in the catalogues as E-gas), and the Motronic ME 7.2 that worked alongside it. This meant horsepower and torque ratings were no different to the regular Carrera's, and gearbox ratios were also the same. However, due to the need to send power to the front axle, the transmission design was different, prompting new code numbers – G96/30 for the manual six-speed unit, and A96/30 for the five-speed Tiptronic.

Whilst the interior was usually the

continued page 99

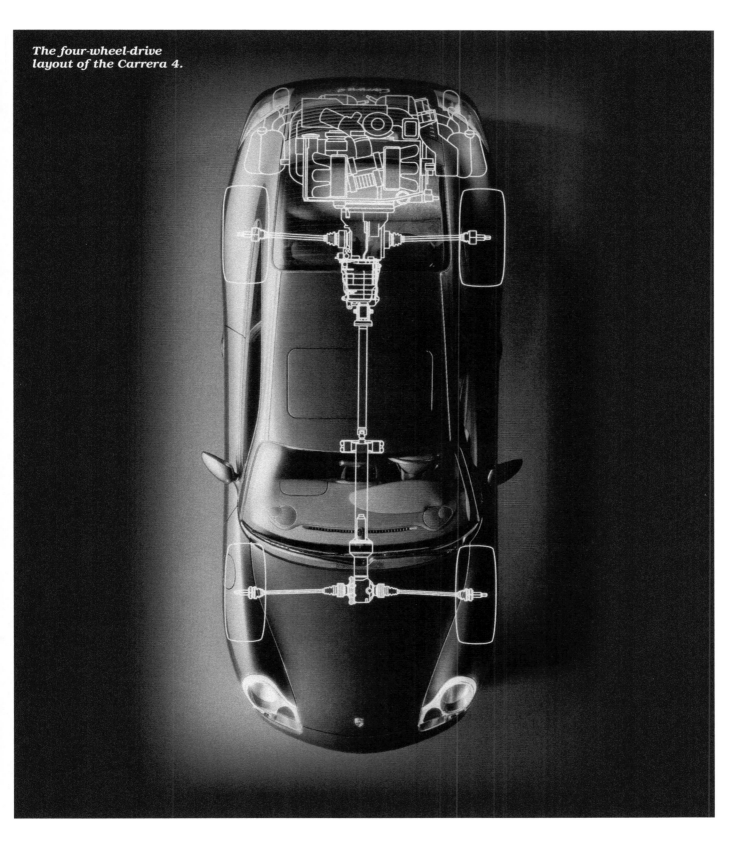

The four-wheel-drive layout of the Carrera 4.

Below: The Tiptronic S gearbox for the C4 (Type A96/30).

Above: The manual gearbox for the C4 (Type G96/30).

The Carrera 4 Cabriolet viewed from the front and rear (overleaf).

A C4 coupé photographed near Lake Garda in Italy. The four-wheel-drive system was designed for better stability rather than enhanced grip, but there was no doubt that the Carrera 4 had an advantage over its RR stablemate in conditions like this.

same as that of the RR Carrera (except for a 'PSM OFF' button replacing the 'TC OFF' one on the centre console, when fitted), detail changes for the C4 included a 'Carrera 4' badge on the tail in silver (titanium in Porsche terminology) rather than the regular car's black, brake calipers finished in silver instead of black, and unique M399 17in five-spoke wheels (albeit with the same rim size as the rear-wheel-drive model and shod with the same rubber); wheel centres gained 'Carrera 4' markings, as did the treadplates on the sills.

In summary, the main advantages of the strict Carrera, of course, were its lighter weight (55kg/121lb less than the C4), larger luggage compartment, greater simplicity, and cheaper sticker price. The Carrera 4 gave the driver the feeling of enhanced security and handling that could be explored in greater safety, especially at higher speeds. Opinion amongst the racing set was divided: Mario Andretti preferred the rear-wheel-drive model, while Hurley Haywood fell for the C4. Walter Rohrl also went for the Carrera 4, exclaiming: "It is just fantastic!"

The X51 engine power enhancement option became available at this time, its modified cylinder head and different intake and exhaust system (plus detail changes to the crankcase and oil pump) taking horsepower up to 320bhp

continued page 106

Standard coachwork colours (1999)
Black, Glacier White, Guards Red, and Pastel Yellow.

Metallic coachwork colours (1999)
Black Metallic, Arctic Silver Metallic, Vesuvio Grey Metallic, Arena Red Metallic, Ocean Blue Metallic, Zenith Blue Metallic, Ocean Jade Metallic, and Mirage Metallic.

Special coachwork colours (1999)
Polar Silver Metallic, Slate Grey Metallic, Violet Metallic, Dark Blue, Cobalt Blue Metallic, Iris Blue Metallic, Midnight Blue Metallic, Wimbledon Green Metallic, Forest Green Metallic, and Speed Yellow.

Cabriolet hood colours (1999)
Black, Graphite Grey, Space Grey, and Metropol Blue.

Trim colours & materials (1999)
Black, Graphite Grey, Space Grey, Metropol Blue or Savanna Beige vinyl, with Black, Graphite Grey, Space Grey, Metropol Blue or Savanna Beige leather as an option; special leathers included Boxster Red or Nephrite. Carpets came in Black, Graphite Grey, Space Grey, Boxster Red, Metropol Blue, Nephrite or Savanna Beige.

A stunning series of shots showing a 1999 Carrera Cabriolet on the move.

The 1999 model year Carrera coupé.

Some alternative ideas for the 996 interior, as shown in the home market's 1999 model year 'Exclusive & Tequipment' catalogue. Note that the white-faced gauges came with indicator and high beam warning lights in the upper part of the tachometer. The high performance audio system was readily identified by larger door speaker enclosures.

911

Various shots showing contemporary 911 production at the Porsche factory. It took an average of 45 hours to build a 996 – a 40 per cent reduction in time compared to putting a 993 together, largely due to a number of components being supplied as built-up modules rather than individual parts. Interestingly, while the Boxster was produced in both Germany and Finland, Marchart stated that the 911 had to be built in Zuffenhausen.

at 6600rpm, and increasing torque output to 265lbft at 5000rpm. Initially only available on the rear-wheel-drive Carrera, the option spread to the C4 as well the following year. Those interested in more power may also have taken a shine to the rollcage or six-point racing harness being offered for fast road use.

Of more general interest was the three-piece, ten-spoke 18in 'Sport Design' wheel option (XRL), plus things like wheel spacers, locking wheelbolts, valve caps with the Porsche crest, and approved snowchains. The 17in 'Sport Classic' rim (XRA) was also listed in some countries, although it was always a more popular choice for the Boxster than the 996.

Litronic lights, a rain sensor pack and automatic dimming mirrors (exterior and/or interior) kept gadget freaks happy, and the centre console on the tunnel could now be trimmed in wood or carbonfibre (or painted silver or body colour), in addition to the existing leather option in a single or deviating colour. Instrument dials could be finished to match the interior colour, and there were more three-spoke steering wheel options, mirroring the trim variations offered on the four-spoke version. Personalized treadplates could also be ordered.

American review

F1 and CART superhero, Mario Andretti, was called in by *Road & Track* to evaluate the handling behaviour of a number of top sports cars, including the C4 coupé, Honda NSX, Dodge Viper, Chevrolet Corvette, Lotus Esprit and Ferrari F355 Spider. In his opinion, the Porsche came out tops, narrowly beating the Honda, but finishing convincingly clear of the others. The German and Japanese entries were neck-and-neck on most things, and it's interesting to note that both scored a perfect ten in the fun-to-drive category – the only models to do so.

Motor Trend looked at a similar group of vehicles (C4 coupé, NSX, Viper and Corvette, plus a Ferrari 550 Maranello, Mercedes-Benz E55 and BMW M Coupé) and put them through their paces in a series of tests. The classic 0-100-0 test was included, and, surprisingly, the Porsche did not do well, finishing last but one. It did much better in the slalom, and on the road.

As Rik Paul observed: "Test numbers tell only part of the story. The Porsche offers its own unique driving experience, one that still generates cult passion. It's the visceral sensation of its 3.4-litre flat-six spooling up a few feet behind your head as you launch it with asphalt-blurring abandon, thanks to the sophisticated all-wheel-drive system. It's that welded to a rail feeling as it straightens out a twisty back road. And the sure-footed high-speed control as it explores the increasingly tenuous terrain above 150mph. It's 'mere' 169.9mph top and 5.0 second 0-60 blitz kept it off the winner's podium in this illustrious event, but at this level of performance ultimate boasting rights often come down to splitting hairs. Besides, from a seat of the pants perspective, the Carrera 4 was easily the most controllable, stable, and comfortable with the speedo needle buried deep into triple digits."

It was also noted that the $70,480 C4, which came with traction control as standard in the States, was "a blast to drive at real world speeds," and a practical proposition as an everyday car. While the Ferrari was a runaway winner (but at nearly three times the price of the 911, anything less would have been unforgivable), on balance, the Porsche came third, just behind its similarly priced Stuttgart rival.

Anyway, at least 1999 saw a further improvement in American sales, the 911 accounting for 8194 of the 20,875 Porsches sold in the States that year (7547 911s had been sold in the previous year, a 26 per cent improvement on 1997 figures). Prices ranged from $65,030 for the strict manual Carrera up to $79,920 for the convertible C4 Tiptronic S, incidentally.

Other major export markets

In England, the 1998 Motor Show was held at the NEC from 22 October to 1 November. Porsche was in Hall 3, with the new Carrera 4 taking pride of place, although this was also the first appearance of the 996 Cabriolet at a UK motor show. In fact, Carrera and C4 versions were on display,

The Porsche stand at the 1998 Paris Salon.

Engine
カレラ パワーキット

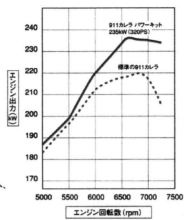

240
230
220
210
200
190
180
170

エンジン出力（kW）

911カレラ パワーキット
235kW (320PS)

標準の911カレラ

5000 5500 6000 6500 7000 7500

エンジン回転数 (rpm)

標準のカレラより、チューニングされたシリンダーヘッド、吸排気系、リフト量が
拡大された専用カムシャフト、そしてモディファイされたコンピュータユニットにより、
エンジンパワーを221kW (300PS) /6,800rpmから235kW (320PS) /6,600rpmへ、
トルクを350Nm (35.7kgm) /4,600rpmから360Nm (36.7kgm) /5,000rpmへと
高めています。また最高速度は、287km/h*を実現。このパッケージには、
強化されたオイル潤滑システムおよびアディショナル ラジエーターが含まれています。
このエンジン性能の拡大とスポーティーなエンジン特性の実現により、
ドライビングプレジャーはいちだんと増しています。*数値は、メーカー発表値による参考値です。

Chassis
スポーツシャシー

バネ定数の高いショートスプリングを装着することにより、全高を
911カレラより10mm低く設定。スタビライザーバーは直径が大きく、
コーナーでの車体の安定性をいっそう高めます。
チューニングしたショックアブソーバーは、路面の感覚をより正確に伝え、
ダイレクトなスポーツフィールを愉しめます。

The Japanese 911 Carrera 'Power Up Edition' of 1999.

Exterior
カップ エアロキット

ポルシェ カレラカップおよびスーパーカップで使用を目的に、
風洞実験を重ねて開発されたのが、この空力パーツです。
構成はスポイラー一体型フロントセクション、サイドスカート、
および複翼式のリアスポイラーです。
エアロダイナミクスの向上だけでなく、外観を楽く、精悍に引き立てます。

Interior
アルミカラー メータパネル

メータパネルは、よりスポーティーな、より機能的な雰囲気を醸し出す、
アルミカラーを採用しました。

3本スポークステアリングホイール

エアバッグを組み込んだスポーツタイプのブラックレザー3本スポーク・
ステアリングホイール。アルミカラー メータパネルともよくマッチし、
よりスポーツマインドを高めてくれます。

スポーツシート

レーシーな雰囲気を高める、本革スポーツシートです。
横方向のサポートを含めて、体のホールド性は抜群です。
前端および高さの調節は手動式、リクライニングも電動です。
さらにバックレストには、エクスクルーシブなポルシェならではのポルシェの
象徴であるクレストがエンボス加工され、プレスティッジアスな
ムードを漂わせます。

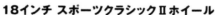

18インチ スポーツクラシックⅡ ホイール

ポルシェ伝統のモータースポーツ活動よりヒントを得た、
18インチ、2ピース構造のアルミホイール。
この独特のY字スポークは、'98ル・マン優勝の911GT1と
同じデザインを採用。卓越した剛性はもちろん、
究極のスポーツ性を象徴しています。

リトロニック ヘッドライト

ヘッドライトは、ガスディスチャージ式。照射範囲が広く、通常の
ハロゲンランプの約2倍もの明るさが特長です。そのため、
夜間走行の疲労は大きく軽減されます。このヘッドライトには、
ヘッドライトウォッシャーと、ダイナミック光軸調整システムが
装備されます。

along with the equivalent coupés, the Boxster, and the Le Mans-winning GT1/98 (not to mention a selection of Porsche bicycles).

Initially, prices were carried over from the previous season at PCGB's 30 dealers, although once the C4 began to filter through, the Cabriolet went up by £150. Carrera 4 prices started at £68,000 for the coupé, with Tiptronic adding £3300 (as on the strict Carrera), and the drophead body adding £6800. To put that into perspective, the Boxster was priced at £34,100 at the time.

Autocar brought together an interesting group of vehicles for a comparison test at the end of 1998 – the new C4 coupé, a Nissan Skyline GT-R, a Subaru Impreza 22B-STi Type UK, and a Mitsubishi Lancer Evolution V. While the magazine felt the C4 was "better than the Carrera 2 in every way," it was outgunned on

The GT3 on display at the 1999 Geneva Show.

Front and rear views of the limited production 911 GT3, which had journalists searching for new superlatives. Those who had complained that the 996 was too cosseting were quickly silenced and returned to the Porsche fold.

this occasion by the hugely talented Japanese cars, coming last in the group, largely due to the value for money factor.

Fuel consumption and prestige apart, it was difficult to justify the price of the Porsche, when the limited edition Subaru and the Mitsubishi cost the same when bought together as a pair, and it was the 'LanEvo' that came out ahead. However, PCGB was allocated 1200 Carreras and 800 C4s for the 1999 season, and there was no lack of takers.

In Japan, the 1999 model year coupé was still priced at 9,900,000 yen, with the C4 commanding 1,000,000 yen more (making it a similar price to the new Jaguar XKR). Regular rear-wheel-drive Cabriolets were listed at 11,500,000 yen, with the C4 version at 12,500,000 yen; Tiptronic S transmission added 800,000 yen on all cars. Interestingly, only the automatic coupés were offered with lhd or rhd, all other grades came in lhd only.

The so-called Comfort package was 1,550,000 yen and included traction control, Litronic headlights (with washers), a rear wiper, power sunroof, leather trim, power seats with heating, lumbar support and driver's-side memory facility, a Porsche crest on the headrests, an onboard computer, and self-dimming rearview mirror; the Sport package was 1,100,000 yen extra and came with the M030 suspension, traction control, a coloured Porsche emblem on the wheel centres, Litronic headlights (with washers), stainless exhaust trim, a rear wiper, Sport seats with leather trim and heating, a Porsche crest on the headrests, stainless treadplates, a black leather-trimmed three-spoke steering wheel, white-faced gauges, an onboard computer, and a self-dimming rearview mirror.

January 1999 saw the launch of the so-called 911 Carrera 'Power Up Edition' in Japan. Limited to 25 cars, the 12,450,000 yen machine, based on the six-speed rear-wheel-drive coupé, came with a tuned engine (the X51 option), the XAA body kit, Litronic light units, Sport Classic II wheels, Sport suspension, white-faced gauges

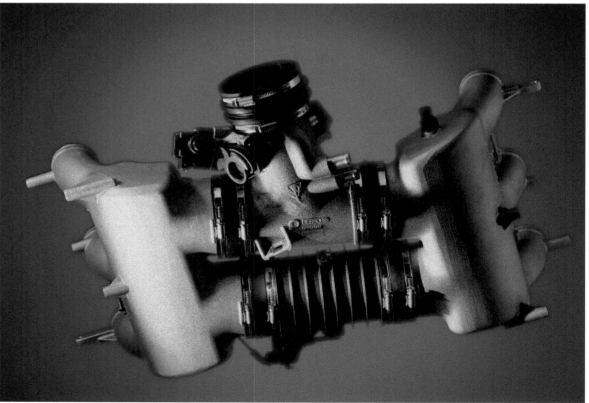

Engine of the GT3 (above), with a close-up of the induction system (right).

Uprated gearbox of the GT3.

beyond a three-spoke steering wheel, and Sport seats with the Porsche crest embossed in the headrest.

In Australia, the 996 Cabriolet arrived at the end of 1998, bringing with it an all-996 line-up to go with the Boxster. The 996 coupé was up to $184,200 by this time, while the drophead was introduced at $199,900. The C4 cost $205,000 with a tin top, or $222,600 in Cabriolet guise; Tiptronic added $8000 to all 911s. The Aussie range was still the same, with prices carried over, going into the 2000 season.

The 1999 Geneva Show
The 1999 Geneva Show ran from 11-21 March, and the star of the Porsche stand was undoubtedly the GT3 road car, introduced as an early 2000 model. While it looked attractive and purposeful, for sure, the GT3's most striking feature was its engine – the M96/76 unit.

The GT3 engine used the same 100 x 76.4mm bore and stroke measurement as the last air-cooled engine to give a 3600cc capacity. In fact, the architecture was similar to the GT1/98 unit – a sort of cross between the 993 and 996 powerplant, with separate cylinder barrels and no crank carrier as on the earlier

car, but featuring water-cooling. The nitride-hardened crankshaft played host to titanium conrods and lightweight pistons, hollow camshafts were used, and there was a reprieve for the traditional 911 dry sump, with capacity increased from 11.1 litres (2.4 imperial gallons) up to 12.5 litres (2.7 gallons) and including no less than six pick-up points to prevent oil surge during extreme cornering.

Delivering 360bhp and 273lbft of torque, the unit was said to be incredibly flexible, but certainly at its best once the needle on the tachometer swung past the 12 o'clock position, which is when the car's variable valve timing (with hydraulically-adjusted camshaft positioning on the GT3) became more noticeable.

The six-speed manual gearbox (Type G96/90) was cable operated, but based on the GT2 transmission for quick repairs or cog changes. Standard internal ratios were 3.82 on first, 2.15 on second, 1.56 on third, 1.21 on fourth, 0.97 on fifth and 0.82 on top (the Japanese spec gearbox, Type G96/93, had slightly different ratios on third and fourth), with the final-drive set at 3.44:1. The GT3 came with an uprated clutch, a GKN limited-slip differential, and an oil cooler for the transmission.

To keep everything in check, the GT3 came with bigger brakes (330mm/13.0in in diameter at both ends, although 34mm/1.3in wide up front and 28mm/1.1in wide at the rear), massive red Brembo four-pot calipers, and a new brake master cylinder to suit the revised ABS system. Adjustable shocks and anti-roll bars were specified, the latter hollow to save weight, but the suspension, although 30mm (1.2in) lower, was not as harsh as former road racers, thanks to Bob Wollek's input. Bigger front wheel bearings and stronger track rod ends were used, as well as harder bushes throughout, but the steering was standard 996 issue.

The Cup body kit was employed, minus the rear valance extensions but with a 'GT3' badge on the tail, complemented by 18in Sport Design wheels: The 8J rims at the front and 10Js at the rear were shod with 225/40 and 285/30 Pirelli rubber.

Moving inside, lightweight bucket seats with leather facings saved 20kg (44lb), and air conditioning and audio equipment became a no-cost option, also in the interest of saving weight. The rear seating was deleted to save another 8kg (18lb), and fuel tank capacity increased to 90 litres (19.8 imperial gallons), leaving no room for a spare wheel, but at least 13kg (29lb) was saved in this way, too. Gauges were virtually the same, except for the tachometer – marked up to 8800rpm, with the red-line at 7600 (200rpm before the limiter cut-in), and a GT3 logo to match the one on the handbrake and treadplates. Incidentally, a 50Ah battery was fitted unless the NCO items were specified.

Oddly, the road car was actually slightly heavier than a regular Carrera,- in order to keep insurance companies happy from a safety angle, and after allowing for a stronger body and a level of equipment expected in today's market. Although a touch noisier than the stock 996, due to reduced sound deadening material, it was far more refined than the old RS or GT2, mainly thanks to nice damper tuning, which consequently made it far more suitable for normal road use in standard guise. Nonetheless, the GT3 was officially capable of 187mph (299kph) and covering the 0-60 dash in 4.6 seconds, so it was certainly no slouch.

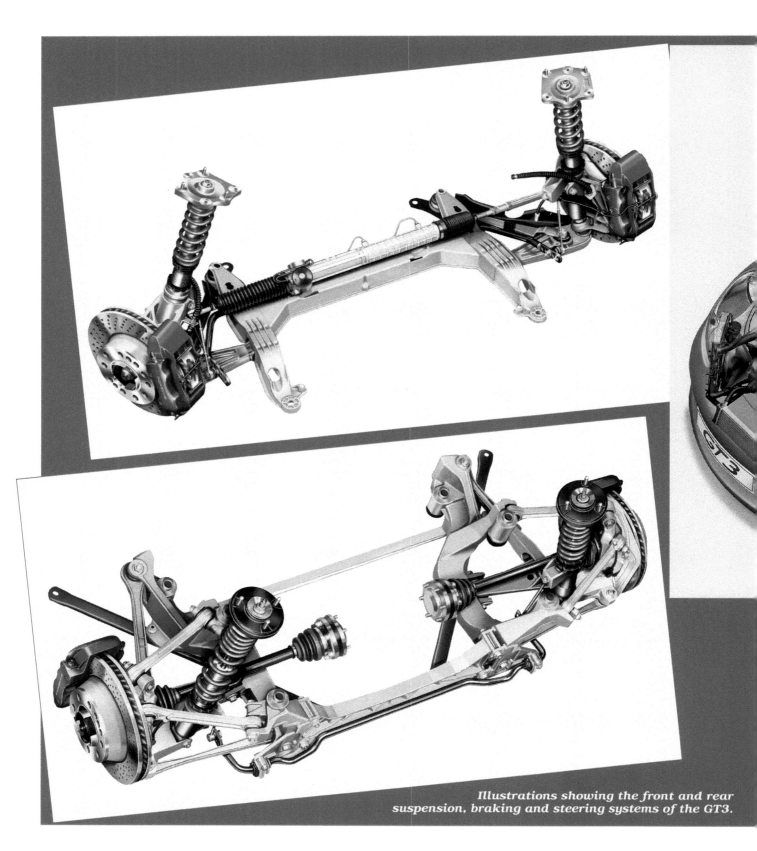

Illustrations showing the front and rear suspension, braking and steering systems of the GT3.

114

Cutaway drawing of the GT3 showing the engine and transmission layout, plus the extensive cooling system incorporating a third radiator in the centre of the front air intake.

Cockpit of the GT3. Although the new model evoked memories of the old RS in the way it handled and responded to driver input, when it came to interior appointment it was certainly more civilized than its illustrious predecessor.

The Club Sport version came with an uprated clutch assembly on a lightened flywheel, an integrated rollcage to replace the standard side airbags, racing-style seats, plus an extinguisher system and battery cut-off, and was 145kg (319lb) lighter, ready to race. 1350 examples were to be built, priced at DM 175,000 apiece, whether in road or Club Sport trim. Unfortunately, the GT3 was not certified for use in the USA, although there was no restriction on importing racing versions.

1999 competition update

Although the company issued an off-the-peg 420bhp GT3R for private teams, Porsche officially took the

For those who loved the aggressive styling but lived in a country where the model wasn't sold, it was possible to make the regular Carrera look like a GT3 with the official factory body kit.

The GT3R of Patrick Huisman, Uwe Alzen and Luca Riccitelli at Le Mans in 1999. A final position of 13th overall gave the team a Class 3 victory.

year off from racing, with no works team entries expected until at least 2000. Rumours of a 650bhp normally-aspirated V8-engined 911 lookalike racer spread around the industry but, in the meantime, that left Le Mans open for Mercedes-Benz, Toyota and BMW. Porsche's Stuttgart neighbour had serious problems with cars becoming airborne whilst slipstreaming, and Toyota's ill fortune on the event ultimately handed victory to the Williams-built BMW.

Across the Atlantic, the American Le Mans Series, which took the place of IMSA events on the race calendar, attracted large fields and provided motorsport fans with some close racing. Cort Wagner won the ALMS driver's title in the GT Class, with Martin Snow's GT2 coming third in GTS. Porsche claimed maker's honours in both, and came fourth in the Prototype category.

In the USRRC series, Porsche won the GT2 and GT3 categories; Larry Schumacher and fellow 911 driver, John O'Steen, tied for the GT2 title,

and Cort Wagner won GT3. Wagner certainly had a good year, as he won the Porsche Cup, too.

The FIA GT Championship lost some of its pizzazz following the withdrawal of Porsche and Mercedes, with GT2 becoming the core element in the series: The Chrysler Viper GTS-R proved to be the car to beat. Meanwhile, the International Sports Racing Series (ISRS), founded in 1997, became the Sports Racing World Cup (SRWC) in 1999, stealing a lot of the limelight from the GT Championship. Porsches were rarely seen on the grid, however, and the Ferrari 333SP dominated the season, as it had in 1998.

The JGTC had no GT500 runners – it was virtually impossible to compete with the specialist racers produced by the Japanese manufacturers. No fewer than ten 911s competed in the GT300 category, but failed to shine on this occasion.

The 2000 model year
At the 1999 Frankfurt Show, which

The sister car to the Class 3 winner, driven by Bob Wollek, Dirk Muller and Bernd Maylander, came a creditable 19th, but 73 laps down on the winning BMW.

ran from 16-26 September, Hall 5 was buzzing with excitement, as Porsche launched the Boxster S and displayed an all-new 3.6-litre 911 Turbo. According to Harm Lagaay, the fast return on 986/996 development costs allowed Porsche to go to town on the Turbo, giving the turbocharged machine its own distinctive character. Without doubt, the investment proved worthwhile once the car went on sale in the spring as an early 2001 model.

Meanwhile, the Carreras benefited from a number of improvements, including a new engine (the M96/04), which was used to power both the strict Carrera and the C4. Although horsepower and torque ratings were officially unchanged from the earlier M96/01 and M96/02 units, the M96/04 featured an E-gas throttle,

117

Various views of the 1999 GT3R – the vehicle that revived Porsche's past glories with road-based competition machinery. With lightweight panels and 420bhp on tap, it proved a very effective GT racer.

modified fuel injectors, and a new crankshaft, air injection pump, auxiliary drive belt tensioner housing, alternator (and pulley), plus a new exhaust system. In addition, the X51 power kit was now available across the Carrera range.

Transmissions were carried over, albeit with a new clutch release bearing for the manual gearbox, modified front driveshafts for the C4, and a revised selector mechanism for the Tiptronic gearbox. At the same time, the lsd/traction control option for the strict RR Carrera was replaced by option M476 – PSM for rear-wheel-drive cars.

As a matter of interest, the M476 option used the pre-charging hydraulic pump from the C4's braking system, while the brake master cylinder was changed to the C4 type for all cars. The brake fluid reservoir was also modified, along with several brake lines, and the C4's brake calipers shortly after the season started; the handbrake lever mechanism didn't escape attention either. Anti-roll bar tie bars were revised at both ends, the steering track rod ends were

Standard coachwork colours (2000)
Black, Biarritz White, Guards Red, and Speed Yellow.

Metallic coachwork colours (2000)
Black Metallic, Arctic Silver Metallic, Vesuvio Grey Metallic, Arena Red Metallic, Ocean Blue Metallic, Zenith Blue Metallic, Rainforest (Jungle) Green Metallic, and Mirage Metallic.

Cabriolet hood colours (2000)
Black, Graphite Grey, Space Grey, and Metropol Blue.

Trim colours & materials (2000)
Black, Graphite Grey, Space Grey, Metropol Blue or Savanna Beige vinyl, with Black, Graphite Grey, Space Grey, Metropol Blue or Savanna Beige leather as an option; special leathers included Natural Dark Grey, Boxster Red, Nephrite or Natural Brown. Carpets came in Black, Graphite Grey, Space Grey, Natural Dark Grey, Boxster Red, Metropol Blue, Nephrite, Natural Brown or Savanna Beige.

German advertising from 2000.

Wenn Sie gerade keine Lust haben,
Rennen zu gewinnen,
fahren Sie mit ihm zur Arbeit.

Der 911 Carrera.

The 911 interior received a subtle facelift for the 2000 season.

Dramatic publicity shot showing the Carrera Cabriolet, priced at DM 158,340 in Germany during the early part of 2000.

The 911 Carrera
The 911 Carrera Cabriolet
The 911 Carrera 4
The 911 Carrera 4 Cabriolet

The 911 Carrera Cabriolet

Press a button. That's all it takes to begin stirring your senses. Upon command, the Cabriolet top quickly glides beneath the rear deck lid, revealing a rush of sensations as you ride the wind at speed. A tap on the accelerator offers another kind of revelation: the classic sound and road-gripping feel of a rear-mounted 911 engine that exploits the rewards of open-topped driving to the fullest. Allowing you to revel in the immediacy of the wide-open road. The wide-open sky. And the wide-open possibilities of piloting a Porsche.

The 911 Carrera

Timeless in its appearance. Single-minded in its purpose. The 911 Carrera is a collection of technical leaps that communicates its intentions with absolute clarity. A 300-hp 3.4 liter engine pours power onto the pavement, while massive four-piston cross-drilled disc brakes reign with equal ease. Force-sensitive power steering works with a lightweight multi-link suspension to command crisp, disciplined handling throughout the 6-speed manual or 5-speed Tiptronic S dual transmission range, while an ergonomically refined interior ensures your journey is as soothing as it is exhilarating.

The 911 Carrera 4

Sporting the most advanced drive system ever on a Porsche road car, the Carrera 4, available in both coupe and cabriolet models, matches uncompromised performance with unparalleled control. The unshakable sense of confidence you feel flows from a full-time all-wheel drive system that intensifies the manual or Tiptronic S performance experience. Leading the charge is a ... traction at all four cor-

The 911 pages from the American range brochure for the 2000 season. Note the buffers on the rear bumper, situated on each side of the registration plate.

changed, and there was a new steering column and PAS pump pulley. The rear crossmember was also modified for the 2000 season.

Interior surfaces were given soft-touch paint to project an image of enhanced quality, and the rooflining and sunvisors were revised on the coupé for the same reason. Plastic seat trim components were colour matched with trim instead of being dark grey only; gearknobs were revised; the active carbon cockpit air filtration system was made standard, and the rear seats gained child seat attachments.

The standard 911 Carrera coupé now cost DM 145,140 on the home market; the C4 was priced at DM 171,770, and the GT3 at DM 179,500. In reality, though, few cars, if any, were ever sold at list price, as there were so many options to choose from.

Cover from the German 'Selection' catalogue, showing a Carrera in the wind tunnel at Weissach. Note the body kit and Porsche bicycle on the roof rack. By the time the 20th century drew to a close, owners were able to order just the XAA aero kit's side skirts (X76) and rear valance flares (XAD), without having to purchase the full set of aerodynamic appendages.

Some alternative Carrera interiors from the US 2000 model year catalogue, two in maple burr (dark and light variations shown), and one with the overtly sporting carbonfibre treatment. Trying to define what was or wasn't standard had become all but impossible by this time ...

In addition to the existing extras, for the 2000 season there were new carbon, leather and maple burr trim packages that extended to fewer components than those originally advertised, and more minor trim items could be specified in leather, allowing the owner to have almost every surface covered in hide! Interestingly, the cloth seat inlay alternative was no longer available by this time. The hood over the instrument pack could be specified in a different colour to the rest of the fascia, however, as could the upper and lower dash sections; the instrument surround could be painted silver, too, for those wanting something a little unusual.

Stateside news

George W Bush took Bill Clinton's place in the White House in 2000, but, on the Porsche front, there wasn't much to report on in America, as the press tended to concentrate on the forthcoming Turbo, often at the expense of outlining the meaningful changes applied to the rest of the 911 range.

Anyway, the 2000 Carrera coupé was listed at $65,590, with a $74,970 sticker price for the soft-top version. The C4 coupé was $71,020, with the Cabriolet commanding $80,400; Tiptronic transmission added $3420 on all cars.

Porsche sales in the US amounted to 22,410 units for 2000 – an increase of around 7 per cent on 1999. The Boxster accounted for 13,312 of these sales, with the 911 making up the balance (9098 units, including the $89,000 'Millennium Special' described in the next section).

The right-hookers

There was the usual display of Porsches at Earls Court in late October, and visitors were also able to get a sneak preview of the mighty Turbo. While the Boxster provided entry-level Porsche motoring from a reasonable £34,232, 911 prices started at £60,271 for the basic rear-wheel-drive Carrera coupé. The Cabriolet body added around £7000, and Tiptronic a further £3300. For those who wanted a car with "a bigger heart and harder fists," there was always the GT3, listed at £76,655, but limited to only 40 copies for the UK market.

In Japan, prices and

The Porsche stand at the 1999 Tokyo Show, with the C4 Cabriolet nearest the camera and the new 911 Turbo in the background.

specifications were carried over from the 1999 season, although, as elsewhere, the C4 'Millennium Special' limited edition was announced in December 1999. Based on the Carrera 4, it came with special Violettchromaflair paintwork, polished Turbo Look wheels, the M030 suspension upgrade, Natural Brown leather trim with dark wood and striped Alcantara accents, and a numbered '911' badge on the centre console. Japan received just 18 of the 911 cars marketed worldwide.

Meanwhile, *Car Graphic* sampled a C4 Cabriolet, and found it to be a very refined sports car, with fine chassis balance and excellent brakes. Wind control in and around the cockpit was also good, rendering the windblocker virtually unnecessary at Japanese road speeds.

As for Australia, the 911 line-up was much the same until the addition of the GT3 at the start of the 2000 model year, and remained that way until August 2000. The GT3 was introduced at $224,600 in Touring or

Club Sport guise, and, as *Wheels* said: "Engine, gearbox, chassis, tyres and brakes come together in a delightful symphony, on road or race circuit. Limits are extraordinarily high and the GT3 remains poised way beyond the point where the RS Club Sport would get untidy ... It's a tough guy car with a soft, emotional side. A New Ager. On cue, the GT3 will perform like a racing car on the track, and then behave like a lamb off it."

Japanese advertising for the GT3, issued shortly after the vehicle's launch.

A Japanese advert from spring 2000, this piece promoting the Carrera 4 coupé. The 17in wheels illustrated here were standard fare for the C4.

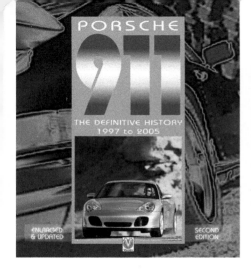

5

A new turbocharged era begins

The Porsche 911 Turbo once again taking centre stage. One had been spotted during testing at Nardo on Monaco Grand Prix weekend, before its public debut.

"The days when '911 Turbo' was another way of saying 'ultimate supercar' are becoming distant now. Porsche has felt the heat from Ferrari, whose 360 makes our hearts beat faster than a 911, and the pressure can only get worse when the Mercedes-McLaren SLR arrives in 2003. Then again, maybe it's the competition that should be worrying about looking bad. No car maker knows how to 'up the ante' like Porsche. And far from being just another pumped-up 911, the latest Turbo is arguably the company's greatest car since the 959 ... It could well be the supercar that sets the pace for the new millennium." – *Autocar***, October 1999.**

The name 'Porsche' and the word 'turbo' somehow seem to go hand-in-hand. Ever since the mid-1970s, it was unthinkable not to have a 911 Turbo in the Stuttgart maker's line-up, despite attempts to kill it off on several occasions. For a generation of enthusiasts, though, the essence of the turbocharged 911 was so strong that it could never be allowed to fade away. Consequently, the 1999 Frankfurt Show witnessed the announcement of a new 996 version. This was followed by a tour of the 1999 European and

Japanese show circuit before the car's official introduction at the 2000 Geneva Show.

A new Turbo

At the heart of any 911 Turbo is the engine, and the latest car was no exception. Basically, the Turbo was powered by the GT3's dry-sump 24v six equipped with twin KKK turbochargers with integral wastegates (carried over from the previous generation), and with intercoolers mounted to the sides rather than the top of the engine, as had been the practice on earlier production Turbos. Maximum boost was set at 11.4psi at 2700rpm, and almost all contemporary reports noted a complete lack of turbo-lag.

The M96/70 unit was given a stronger crankshaft, but steel conrods (the GT3 used titanium items in keeping with its racing roots). Bosch Motronic ME 7.8 replaced the ME 7.2 version employed on the regular Carreras, and the variable valve timing system was significantly improved, being based on that of the GT3, with a hydraulic attachment on the intake camshafts rather than tensioning the timing chain, to give a far greater degree of position adjustment. In addition, Variocam Plus, as it was called, ditched the regular camshaft

Harm Lagaay talking to the press regarding the styling of the latest Turbo. Pinky Lai was responsible for much of the design work.

2700rpm, although the same output was delivered all the way through to 4600, so the unit was very flexible, with excellent mid-range punch. To cope with the extra power, cooling surfaces were 50 per cent greater than those of the regular Carrera; hence the requirement for larger intakes at the front of the vehicle.

The Turbo came with either a six-speed manual or five-speed Tiptronic S gearbox, the latter (Type A96/50) adapting to driver input, and offered on the turbocharged model for the first time. The semi-automatic came with ratios of 3.59 on first, 2.19 on second, 1.41 on third, a direct fourth, and 0.83 on fifth; a 3.44:1 or 3.78:1 final-drive was specified, depending on the market it was intended for.

On the manual transmission (Type G96/50), the hydraulic clutch was made lighter for the driver, thanks to a pressure accumulator working off the PAS pump, as per the 993 Turbo, and a dual-mass flywheel was employed for added refinement. Internal ratios were 3.82 on first, 2.05 on second, 1.41 on third, 1.12 on fourth, 0.92 on fifth and 0.75 on sixth; the final-drive was listed at 3.44:1.

design in favour of one with two lobe profiles per valve, that could operate either independently or simultaneously when locked together by an oil pressure-driven pin. It was all very clever: at low load, the low lift/short duration lobe acted on the valve lifter, whilst high load situations

locked the pin in place and brought the high lift/long duration one into play for enhanced performance.

With a high 9.4:1 compression ratio, the Turbo engine was rated at 420bhp DIN (415bhp SAE nett) at 6000rpm (750rpm short of the limiter), and gave 413lbft of torque at

Front and rear views of the M96/70 power-unit. The X50 option brought an uprated 450bhp/457lbft Turbo engine designated the M96/70E.

The lightweight four-wheel drive system was basically the same as that of the contemporary C4. The Fitchel & Sachs torque distribution system sent power to the wheels with the most traction, with a maximum of 40 per cent going to the front axle in extreme conditions (generally only 5 per cent), thus retaining the car's rear-wheel drive bias.

The suspension was also based on that of the Carrera 4, although it was lowered by 10mm (0.4in) and featured beefier anti-roll bars. The brakes were also uprated, the 330mm (13.0in) diameter discs and red four-pot calipers coming straight off the GT3. Alternatively, during the 2001 season proper, ceramic brake discs were offered as an option (M450), each being 5kg (11lb) lighter than the regular production items. The Turbo continued to employ ABS version 5.7, incidentally, although the PSM system came as standard.

As for wheels and tyres, M415 'Monobloc' 8J x 18 rims with five hollow spokes played host to 225/40 rubber at the front, while 11J x 18 versions were used at the back, shod with 295/30 tyres; the centre caps carried 'Turbo' script in black. Similar wheels with solid spokes – the old M413 Turbo Look design – could be bought separately as an option for the other 911s, or even fitted on the Turbo if the owner wanted to reduce the bottom line on the invoice slightly at the time of purchase. It was also possible to delete the M415 wheel for another 18-inch rim with spacer rings. On the subject of wheels, it should be noted that the anti-theft wheel bolt design was changed at this time.

The latest Turbo was readily distinguished by its new front bumper with three large intakes (protected by black grilles) and a rather subtle lip spoiler; the headlights (Litronic lighting was standard, complete with integral washers) were also revised to put further distance between the NA cars and the turbocharged machine. The rocker panels were flared, angled downward at the back to direct air around more of the tyre, and shaped to smooth out the transition area formed by the standard Carrera door and wider Turbo rear wings. The rear fenders added 60mm (2.4in) to the width of the vehicle (to allow for

Testing airflow over the Turbo's body in the Weissach wind tunnel.

the wider track caused by the new tyre and wheel combination), but otherwise dimensions were pretty much the same as on the Carrera: Apart from suspension changes which reduced height, there was just 5mm (0.2in) of extra length to account for when parking up. There was an intake in the leading edge of each rear wing for the intercoolers (also protected by black grilles), and vents near the exhausts on the rear valance to help draw air through the intercoolers and take heat away from the wastegates. There was a two-piece rear spoiler, with the upper part rising 100mm (4in) once the car's speed reached 75mph (120kph), and this, combined with minimal bodywork changes to the coupé shell, kept the drag co-efficient down to a more than reasonable Cd 0.31.

The slippery shape, 400 plus horsepower, and relatively low weight (1540kg/3388lb for the MT car, with Tiptronic adding 45kg/100lb) combined to endow the Turbo with stunning performance. The official 0-60 time was 4.2 seconds (4.9 for the Tiptronic model), while top speed was quoted as being 190mph (305kph), or 185mph (296kph) for the semi-automatic. The only limiting factor in making seriously rapid progress on the continent was the 64-litre (14.1 Imperial gallon) fuel tank, which tended to limit the vehicle's range somewhat, despite improved economy.

Inside, the Turbo had its own instrument pack with different markings and digital sections (due to the upgraded onboard computer), and came with automatic air conditioning, a ten-speaker sound system, full power adjustment for the seats (with memory facility on the driver's side), full leather trim, and a three-spoke steering wheel. The luggage compartment releases were changed to electromagnetic items, working alongside the remote control on the central locking to open the lids.

The Turbo was introduced as an early 2001 model, and indeed, colour and trim options were as per the 2001 season from the start of production, despite sales beginning from the spring of 2000 in Europe. It was released at DM 234,900 on the domestic market, with individual options and packages similar to those offered on the contemporary Carreras, with the obvious exception of equipment already supplied as standard on the turbocharged car.

Turbo exports

The Turbo was due in the States from June 2000. Like the US Carreras, it came fully loaded (a higher level of standard equipment was specified for American cars compared with those of Europe, including those shipped to the UK by this time), and was announced at just over $110,000.

Sadly, in addition to the now-familiar rubber buffers around the rear number plate, US Turbos were

The new Turbo, officially introduced as an early 2001 model, photographed in Lanzarote in December 1999. Friedrich Bezner was in charge of the project.

blighted by rather unsightly buffers up front, too. Mounted at the top inner corner of the two larger intakes, the rubber appendages got the Turbo past Federal legal requirements, but were hardly pretty and looked like something of an afterthought.

Car & Driver put the manual Turbo up against the Ferrari 360 Modena F1 and the Aston Martin DB7 Vantage to see which was the most impressive. Ultimately, it was the Italian car that won the shoot-out, finishing on 96 points – only one ahead of the German vehicle, while

Litronic lights were standard on the Turbo, with xenon gas discharge lighting for high and low beam. Light direction adjusted automatically when the car was on the move to avoid dazzling oncoming motorists. Note the top blade of the rear spoiler in its raised position.

the British car was eight points adrift at the end of the contest.

The price of normally-aspirated 911 motoring went down in the UK at this time, with the Carrera coupé starting at £55,950; a convertible body adding £6050, and Tiptronic a further £3300. The situation was similar with the C4, the price of entry being £59,650 for a four-wheel drive Carrera, with £6100 extra for a Cabriolet, and £3300 for the semi-automatic

Interior of the Turbo. The speedometer was marked up to 320kph (or 200mph, depending on the market), with the 8000rpm tachometer red-lined at 6600rpm.

The Turbo had a two-piece ducktail spoiler – unusual but very effective. Note the familiar script on the rear panel, given a bright finish for the 996-based car.

The standard wheel and tyre combination for the turbocharged model, with the regular braking system clearly visible through the spokes.

For the ultimate in stopping power the Turbo could be specified with the Porsche Ceramic Composite Brake (PCCB) braking system. The PCCB discs weighed half what a conventional rotor did, elegantly and effectively reducing unsprung weight, and were far more efficient in poor conditions. They were not available straight away, but were offered for the 2001 model year proper.

The Turbo's brakes being put under pressure on a test rig.

transmission. The GT3 was actually a touch more expensive, at £76,835, while the Turbo was introduced at £86,000 (or £89,300 with a Tiptronic gearbox) once deliveries began on the first day of June – almost the cost of three 2.7-litre Boxsters, but still a lot less than the expected £95,000 at the time of its announcement!

Autocar compared the new Turbo to the Ferrari 360 Modena F1 and declared that, even without taking the 911's price advantage into account: "Ferrari's dynamically best sports car is well beaten by the Turbo. Porsche does the unthinkable by putting the 360 in the shade ... It's now soothing enough to be a very effective GT cruiser, yet it's also much more aggressive in character than of old. Porsche has turned the car into a proper Grand Tourer as well as a cutting-edge sports car."

A shot taken at the Turbo's press launch in Carmona, Spain.

An American-spec Turbo undergoing inspection prior to shipment. The unsightly rubber buffers were added in response to Federal regulations, although it appears that many were removed once the car left the showrooms.

The Japanese market received the Turbo in mid-March 2000, priced at 16,800,000 yen. Japanese racing hero Aguri Suzuki tried one against the Ferrari 360 Modena F1 for *Navi* magazine, and declared it an honorable draw. He was surprised at how good the Stuttgart machine was, and liked the fact that it was easy and safe to travel quickly in the 911, but questioned its existence with Porsche already having the GT3 in the line-up. Suzuki-san had owned a 911 Turbo in the past, and declared that he preferred the traditional models with two-wheel drive, and the option of a manual gearbox only.

Interestingly, the same journal pitched various Porsches against the stopwatch at the Tsukuba circuit at the same time, and found that the regular Carrera coupé with manual transmission would go round in 1 min 09.32, with the C4 Cabriolet with Tiptronic only fractionally slower (1 min 10.20). The manual Turbo,

however, completed the course in 1 min 05.92; in other words, mighty quickly!

Another racer, Wayne Taylor, noted: "[The Turbo] has a very comfortable ride. At 300kph-plus with crosswind, I can feel some instability, but it's easily correctable. Under deceleration, while other cars would move a little with turbulence, the Turbo feels rock solid. This car inspires a lot of confidence. As an everyday car, the Porsche has everything that anybody could ever want."

Racing in Y2K

With little opposition, Audi dominated Le Mans, taking the top three places in the French classic in mid-June. At least Porsche was well represented in the GT category: Dick Barbour's GT3R won, only to be disqualified,

but another 911 was next in line to claim the victor's spoils. Then, in the legendary Nürbringring 1000km race (held on 9 July), Porsche 911s dominated the GT Class, although it was a Panoz that ultimately took the chequered flag first.

Meanwhile, the ALMS series had matured into something special, although it was Audi that proved the dominant force over the year. The Grand-Am (Grand American Road Racing) series replaced the USRRC, and Porsche won the GTU category in the season opener at Daytona. Indeed, 911 drivers filled the first four places in the championship at the end of the year, with Mike Fitzgerald claiming overall GTU honours, just ahead of Darren Law. As a manufacturer, Porsche easily won the GTU category, and came third in the GTO Class.

Various shots of Turbo production, from welding through to finished bodies on a conveyor high above Porschestrasse, on their way to the main assembly hall, and the attachment of bumper panels and underbody covers.

The FIA GT Championship went through another difficult year, but came through at the end with a grid full of privateers to replace the missing factory teams, while the SRWC eventually became the FIA Sports Car Championship, giving it greater status.

The FIA GT title duly went to the Jaguar-engined Lister, but Christophe Bouchut and Patrice Goueslard won the N-GT category for Series Grand Touring Cars with their 911 GT3R. Homologation papers were issued for the GT3 on 1 March 2000 (N-GT 02), and were good through to at least 2007.

In the Porsche Cup, Mike Fitzgerald reigned supreme. The 911 GT3 Cup model duly qualified for FIA Grand Touring Cars Class 2 status on April Fool's Day, 1999, incidentally, being the ninth car to be accepted in the GT2 category.

There were still no GT500s in the JGTC, but Porsche was well represented in GT300, the field including 993s and 996s, and even a Boxster. At the end of the season, Hideo Fukuyama was crowned champion, driving a 996 GT3R.

News from Zuffenhausen
Porsche announced record profits, and then hit the headlines in virtually every enthusiast publication when the Carrera GT made its debut at the 2000 Paris Salon. This amazing two-seater was powered by a 558bhp V10 developed for a stillborn Le Mans

racer, and was said to be the prototype of a forthcoming production model. The launch of the new 911 GT2 during the 2001 season was somewhat overshadowed by the arrival of the carbonfibre-bodied open GT, but it was good to see the men at Porsche in such buoyant mood again.

As usual, a series of improvements were outlined for the new season. 2001 model Carreras gained a new crankshaft and timing chain (plus self-adjustment mechanism), and the intermediate shaft on the camshaft received attention again. The fuel injectors were revised, as was the auxiliary drive belt tensioner, and countries with stricter emissions control gained new catalytic converters to go with the 911's latest tailpipes.

Improvements were made to the gearbox mounting plate and selector cable (both MT and AT), while the Tiptronic selector mechanism was modified again. A new clutch release bearing was also adopted on the six-speed models at this time, and all cars benefited from a new handbrake lever mechanism and cable.

The body's roof frame rails were reinforced, and the headlights changed slightly (but not to the extent of the Turbo lights at this stage). Inside was a revised instrument cluster (with indicator and main beam warning lights in the tachometer, as on the white-faced meters). The central locking remote and keylamp was also revised, as was the cupholder – a new design inserted in the centre console

The car that came 13th at Le Mans to take GT Class honours in the 2000 event, but was later disqualified.

just below the air vents replacing the hideous plastic thing used previously. The latter was classed as an option for 2001 (on cars without PCM), but an improved version ultimately came as standard on 2002 models.

The GT3 also received a few modifications for the 2001 season: The valve guides and water pump were

revised, along with the front underbody spoilers around the suspension, and the rear anti-roll bar mounting. The gear selector cable, gearknob and handbrake were different to those of the earlier cars, as were the sunvisors and inner door panels.

In Germany, the basic Carrera coupé was listed at DM 140,940 at the start of the 2001 season, with the four-wheel drive version costing DM 152,100. The GT3 carried a sticker price of DM 181,295, while the 911 Turbo coupé commanded DM 237,250. Prices remained the same as summer approached, although the GT3 disappeared: a victim of strict emissions regulations.

The so-called Aluminium & Chrome package (including stainless steel exhaust trims, steel treadplates, and white-faced instruments) was deleted, although a couple of new set combinations were made available for 2001: The GT Package (with the full body kit, stainless exhaust trim and M030 suspension); the

continued page 144

The GT3R of Hideo Fukuyama, Atsushi Yogo and Bruno Lambert which inherited first place in the GT category at Le Mans after Dick Barbour's car was relegated.

The Porsche Supercup in Monaco, with Bernd Maylander in control.

*Action from the 2000 American
Le Mans series.*

The 911 competing in the British BRDC GT Championship; this picture was taken at the Croft round in April.

Atmospheric shot showing the colourful spectacle provided by the Supercup.

A number of earlier action photographs were retouched for the 2001 model year, the cars being given number plates to freshen up the images. These two pictures show the strict Carrera coupé; the rear view is useful in that it shows the duplicate third brake light on the trailing edge of the spoiler, which was only visible when the rear wing was in the raised position.

Retouched C4 photographs, used by advertising agencies around the world during the 2001 season. An American advert from the time declared: "We don't know who invented speed bumps, but we're pretty sure he wasn't German."

Revised fascia of the 2001 model year Carreras.

The M96/04 engine with the X51 power enhancement goodies, prior to dressing. The different intake manifolds used on the 320bhp unit are an obvious distinguishing feature.

The 2001 C4 Cabriolet at speed. The power hood operation could be triggered by a dash-mounted switch, via the door lock, or by remote control as an option.

The massive selection of interior variations available at this time. This small sample of what was on offer clearly illustrates that 911 trim could be ordered to perfectly comply with an owner's taste – from pure sports to pure luxury, and anything in-between. Here, we can see a Carrera with black bucket seats with blue seatbelts to match the body colour and centre tunnel; another with red leather and carbon trim, and still others with the Arctic Silver Package, dark burr maple accents, ruffled Natural Brown leather and a fairly standard cockpit in grey.

Wolfgang Dürheimer became the head of R&D following Horst Marchart's retirement in the spring of 2001.

Comfort Package (with full power seat adjustment, lumbar adjustment and a memory facility on the driver's side), and the Design Package (with stainless 'Carrera' treadplates and exhaust trim, white-faced gauges, a silver rear console, and an aluminium/leather gearknob and handbrake lever).

In addition, the old Hi-Fi and DSP options were replaced by a new Technic Package, which added Litronic lights (with washers), an onboard computer, and a CD unit to the stereo equipment, plus a Windblocker on drophead models. Also new was the so-called Arctic Silver Interior Trim Package, bringing with it a striking combination of silver paint and black leather accents.

The Porsche Ceramic Composite Brake (PCCB) braking system became available, and the M413 'Turbo Look' wheel could now be specified with a polished finish (M414) as well as the regular dull silver. The 911 Turbo gained a 'Turbo' Aero Kit (XAF), whilst for NA 911s, the 'Carrera' rear spoiler (XAG) was available through the Exclusive programme, suitable for both open and closed cars (the 'Cup' spoiler was listed for the coupé only).

A GT2 in the wind tunnel at Weissach.

It was around this time, in March 2001, that Horst Marchart retired, handing the responsibility of being R&D chief to Wolfgang Dürheimer. Born in 1958, Dürheimer spent most of his career at BMW before moving to Porsche to manage development of the 911 series in 1999.

The GT2

The GT2 made its world debut at the 2001 Detroit Show, as if to compensate the Americans for not getting the GT3. The new model, developed under Hartmut Kristen, was approved for worldwide sales, and production would be limited only by the number of people willing to part with the necessary DM 339,000 required to secure one.

When deliveries began in May 2001, the differences between the GT2 and the regular Turbo – on which it was based – became obvious. The bodywork was more aggressive, with deeper front intakes and the lip spoiler projecting further forwards. There was also a slit at the leading edge of the front lid, which, although far from attractive, played a crucial role in the car's aerodynamics package. Around the back, the GT2 acquired a new rear spoiler with an adjustable angle of attack on the top blade (six positions were provided), and whereas the badge on the tail of the Turbo was in silver, the GT2 version was in black.

Power came from the M96/70S unit. With its different intercoolers, turbochargers and exhaust system, it delivered 462bhp DIN (456bhp SAE nett) at 5700rpm, plus 457lbft of torque at 3500rpm. The transmission (Type G96/88) had the same internal ratios and final-drive as the six-speed Turbo, but came with a GKN

40-65 per cent mechanical lsd and rear-wheel drive only, along with a water/oil heat exchanger to keep the transmission cool. Needless to say, the clutch was uprated to cope with the extra sting in the tail, and, in keeping with its competition roots, optional gear ratios were available.

Most of the chassis changes related to the difference between the Turbo's 4WD versus the GT2's RR layout. There were, therefore, different front wheel carriers, although the bearings and hubs were the same. The suspension was uprated on the GT2 (Bilstein shocks were employed on both turbocharged cars, however), lowered by an extra 20mm (0.79in) and made fully adjustable.

The wheels and tyres looked identical to those of the Turbo, but were, in fact, slightly wider. Up front 8.5J x 18 rims played host to 235/40 rubber, while 12J x 18 alloys were used at the back, shod with 315/30s; there was a Porsche crest in the wheel centre.

Purposeful tail of the GT2. Note the different rear spoiler, although something resembling a subtler version of the larger two-tier wing could be bought through the 'Tequipment' catalogue as an option for other 911 models.

PORSCHE

Exhilaration

The New 911 Turbo

Exhilaration. You can literally see the passion, the exhilaration and the knowledge gained in thousands of grueling races and years of development communicated in the striking design of the new Porsche 911 Turbo. The rear spoiler and aerodynamic profile trace their roots to the Porsche 935 twin turbo, one of the most successful race cars of all time. The Turbo's all-wheel drive evolved from the system first introduced on the groundbreaking

Porsche 959, winner of the Paris to Dakar Rally. While the 420 horsepower flat six was derived directly from the engine that powers the Le Mans winning 911 GT-1 racecar. The simple fact is, every feature of every Porsche, from the sculpting of a wheel spoke to the placement of the tachometer in the center of the instrument cluster, is meticulously engineered with one thing in mind: using everything we've learned to elevate the driving experience to breathtaking new heights. It is this which separates Porsches from other sports cars and binds them together as a family of pure, exhilarating driving machines.

146

Tail of the US-spec Carrera coupé for the 2001 season.

Interior of a Carrera drophead for the US market.

The new Turbo with Federal bumpers.

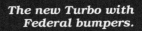

In reality, though, it was what lurked behind the wheels that created the most interest, as the 350mm (13.8in) diameter ceramic brakes were standard on the GT2. It was possible to specify cast steel rotors (M449), but, regardless of the discs, the GT2 came with yellow six-pot calipers at the front and special four-pot versions at the rear. The brake servo and reservoir were different, and the braking system software was unique, too, the GT2 employing version 5.3 ABS instead of 5.7 on all the other 911s.

Weighing in at 1440kg (3168lb) – 100kg (220lb) lighter than a regular Turbo – the GT2 had no rear seats (although there was a GT2 logo on the carpet on the rear firewall to match the one on the treadplates and handbrake lever), and lightweight glassfibre buckets up front, trimmed in leather as standard. Air conditioning was also standard, along with a rain-sensing windscreen, power windows and self-dimming power mirrors, while a stereo was classed as a no cost option. As a result, the GT2 battery was rated at 70Ah, only 10Ah down on the Turbo item.

With a 0-60 time of four seconds dead and a top speed of 196mph/314kph (which can be confirmed by the Italian police, who stopped a journalist for doing this speed during the press launch near Venice), the GT2 was certainly fast. It was fairly frugal, too, given the level of performance, with *Autocar* recording a test average of 16.8mpg for the quasi-racer. With a larger 90-litre (19.8 Imperial gallon) fuel tank, this gave the car quite a useful range.

There was also a Club Sport version of the GT2 equipped with rollcage, bucket seats trimmed in inflammable cloth, red six-point seatbelts (three-point for the passenger), a fire extinguisher, and a battery master cut-off switch. This could be specified as a no cost option.

The US 2001 model year

For 2001, US cars gained a full four-year, 50,000-mile, bumper-to-bumper warranty, in addition to the existing ten-year anti-perforation guarantee on the body. Prices, however, went virtually unchanged, with the NA 911 range starting at $66,500 for the Carrera coupé, and

rising to $111,000 for the Turbo, before options.

The Turbo was the subject of a *Road & Track* test in November 2000, which declared: "The Porsche makes a pleasant, easy-going Interstate cruiser that loafs along with no mechanical noise, but a fairly high level of tyre noise. That slap-slap-slap on road seams can make the excellent sound system less riveting than it might be. Such is the price of seemingly infinite grip.

"Other than that, the Turbo is an extremely civilized touring companion … We had only two complaints with the interior. One is the grey dash top, which reflects badly in the windshield in bright sun, and the other is the lack of lumbar support in the electrically adjustable seats. Adjustable lumbar support is an option."

Toward the end of the year, the events of 11 September 2001 had a devastating effect on trade. Stock prices fell sharply, fuel prices increased, and the general mood was not one of buying luxury goods on impulse. Until then, PCNA had been doing quite well, helping to boost the total 2001 CY sales figure to 23,041 units – up slightly on the previous year. This was made up by 12,278 Boxsters and 10,763 911s.

Rhd market review

John Major had lost the election to Tony Blair in 1997, putting Labour in power for the first time since 1979. Despite a distinct shortfall in delivery of election promises, Blair was re-elected for a second term in June 2001. Meanwhile, Porsche prices and specifications were carried over from the previous season, although the GT3 had disappeared from the price lists by the end of spring.

At the NEC, the Porsche stand (number 3550) featured the Carrera GT, though it was a long time before it was seen at any of PCGB's 30 dealers. The GT2 was the hottest thing available from Zuffenhausen until the GT's launch, and *Autocar* put one in a twin test against the TVR Tuscan S.

The magazine was quite surprised by the GT2's refinement: "For a Porsche wearing a GT moniker, the driving experience and range of sensations it provides via its controls are curiously aloof. It's almost as if the

car's makers decided they didn't want you to know just how damn fast it is, for fear that the news would be too disturbing.

"On the other hand, some things the GT2 can do are quite incredible. Just the way it goes in a straight line without more than a hint of turbo-lag, and the manner in which it stops so quickly and calmly no matter how lumpy the road surface, are unrivalled at any price. And its seats and general driving position are similarly wonderful. With the no-cost option sports seats fitted, it has a cabin that, ergonomically if not aesthetically, feels as if it's been handcrafted around you: Everything fits just so."

But it shouldn't be forgotten that the GT2 was in a comparison test, and the biggest difference – apart from the fact the Porsche cost more than twice as much – was found to be the fun factor: "The Tuscan is a riot at all times; when you're bumbling along at 40mph and when you're flat on the floor doing Mach 3 with your hair on fire. The GT2 only really starts to come alive around the Mach 2 mark, and even then it's not as open with its emotions."

It's interesting to reflect on earlier 911 test reports at this point. The first ones described the car as alert – a living beast, almost. As we moved into the 1970s, more refinement was added, but communication between car and driver remained. More luxury – and weight – became a feature of the 1980s, and effortless performance, as opposed to the high revs action required of the earliest 911s. It was a transition from sports car to Grand Tourer, and now even the most sporting variant of the line was becoming a fast but comfortable cruiser. Of course, purists will always prefer more focused machines, but the market had changed considerably over the years (offering an automatic gearbox in the Turbo was proof of this), and Porsche simply had to move with the times in order to survive.

In Japan, the strict Carrera coupé was 9,900,000 yen, while the C4 version was 10,900,000 yen. In drophead guise, the rear-wheel drive Carrera commanded 11,500,000 yen, with four-wheel drive costing 1,000,000 yen more. The Turbo coupé

Another American brochure, this one from early 2001, with the GT2 as the centre of attention.

GT2

The dream of every driving enthusiast is a racecar for the street. So why not one based on the sports car that won the most prestigious road race in the world? With 456 horsepower, the 911 GT2 is the most powerful road-going 911 ever built. The twin turbo flat-six engine is a derivative of the powerplant that captured first and second place at Le Mans in 1998. The body features lightweight construction and a lower center of gravity. The suspension is fully adjustable for road and track. The brake disks are race-bred carbon fiber. The wind tunnel-honed aerodynamics minimize drag and promote down force. The end result is the ultimate 911, courtesy of the engineers at Porsche Motorsport.

911

PORSCHE

It began with a dream.
And the car built to chase it.

---

was a hefty 16,800,000 yen in basic guise, while Tiptronic S transmission added 800,000 yen to all cars.

In Australia, the 2.7-litre Boxster was priced the same as last season at the start of the 2001 model year, but the 3.2-litre model cost $4100 less. The Carrera was also slightly cheaper, down to $181,900, while the Cabriolet was listed at $197,800, the C4 coupé at $202,900, and the C4 Cabriolet at $220,700; the Turbo had been introduced at $298,800.

Competition update

There was still no factory involvement in top flight racing, other than the Supercup (won in 2001 by Jorg Bergmeister), and that could hardly be classed as true competition. After all, in a one-make series, it's obvious which car is going to win – the Supercup is basically a test of driver skill more than anything else.

The FIA GT Championship went to Chrysler Viper GTS-R pilots, although Porsche notched up an

N-GT Class win at six of the 11 rounds (Monza, Brno, Zolder, Spa, the Nürburgring, and Estoril). Even this was not enough to claim driver's honours in the N-GT category, though, with a Ferrari 360 Modena pairing walking away with the trophy.

Le Mans fell to Audi, although the GT3 of Gabrio Rosa, Fabio Babini and Luca Drudi came a remarkable sixth overall to take a GT Class win. Actually, 996s did well, filling four of the top ten slots – quite something,

GEMBALLA

Legend of Nürburgring

ニュルブルグリングの伝説

GEMBALLA 996 BITURBO GTR 600 / Oct. 2000　ニュルブルグリング ノースコースにてラップタイム 7：44,7*ニューレコードを記録！

The new Top Athlete : GEMBALLA GTR 600
- 650 PS-0-100 in 3,5 sec. -0-200 in 11,5 sec.* Vmax > 340 km/h-
- Lap time Nürburgring (Nordschleife)　7：44, 7*
- Lap time Hockenheim (kleiner kurs)　1：11, 4*

GEMBALLA 996 BITURBO GTR 600 / GTR 500 / GT 500

GEMBALLA USED COMPLETE CAR LINE UP

'98 GEMBALLA 996　¥.ASK
BITURBO GT 500

'97 GEMBALLA 993　¥.ASK
EXTREMO 600

'97 GEMBALLA 993　¥.ASK
Turbo S 520hp

《 お問合せはゲンバラ・ジャパンまで！ 》

DESIGN
Uwe Gemballa
GEMBALLA JAPAN CO.,LTD.　Showroom /Office 〒141-0031
東京都品川区西五反田5-6-43
Tel. 03-3490-6911 Fax.03-3490-6946 http://www.gemballa.co.jp

given the big budget racers of the time, which were often fielded with factory backing.

In the ALMS series, Audi won the top category, with Chevrolet taking the GTS title, and BMW the GT trophy (Porsche's German rival winning with 204 points, with the Stuttgart maker second on 180). Revenge was sweet in the Grand-Am series, however, with Porsche beating BMW (342 to 301) in the GT category, and also nudging out Saleen – by the slim margin of just one point – in the GTS title chase.

There were still only GT300 runners in the JGTC, but 911s made up almost half the field. Unfortunately, this was not enough to guarantee victory, and the title ultimately went to a Nissan Silvia driver. The Carrera Cup Japan was full of 911s, of course, and its popularity reached new heights after its inaugural season in 2001.

Japanese advertising featuring the mighty Turbo.

The GT3 Cup car for the 2001 series, with more power and increased downforce thanks to its larger rear spoiler.

The GT3RS ready to campaign the 2001 season. Improved cooling was provided via a water/oil heat exchanger (as fitted to the GT2), prolonging the life of the car's transmission in endurance events.

153

オイルとガソリンでは、絶対負けない。

Shell advertising from the latter part of 2001, featuring the Team Taisan 996 campaigned in the Japanese Grand Touring Championship. Although 2001 wasn't so good for number 26, the same GT3R had won the 2000 JGTC title in similar livery.

World Championship Grand Prix
Shell Advance Honda

All Japan Grand Touring Car
Championship Team TAISAN Jr. With ADVAN

World Superbike Championship
Ducati Infostrada Ducati L&M

Cart Fedex Championship
Team Rahal

昭和シェル石油
http://www.showa-shell.co.jp/

[Shell Racing for iモード]に参加で豪華賞品！
http://www.showa-shell.co.jp/i (i-mode専用サイト)

Waves of Change

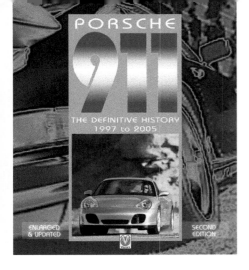

6

Still a star attraction at forty

The death knell had been sounded for the 911 on so many occasions, yet its future looked brighter than ever as it approached its fortieth year in production ...

The normally-aspirated 911s received a new engine and a sharper look, with fresh bumpers and a slightly revised headlight design, the latter being borrowed from the Turbo. This was a useful distinguishing feature for the 911 series, visually distancing it from the Boxster. Other than the body, interior, crossmember and rear control arm modifications adopted on all 911s, there were hardly any changes made to the Turbo or GT2 (new coil springs for the strict Turbo being the most noteworthy by far), although there was now a Turbo lookalike in the form of the new Carrera 4S, along with another novel interpretation of the Targa model. With these additional

The 2002 season brought a new front mask for the venerable Carrera, seen here in standard RR coupé guise. Note the latest smoked front indicator lens near the front wheel.

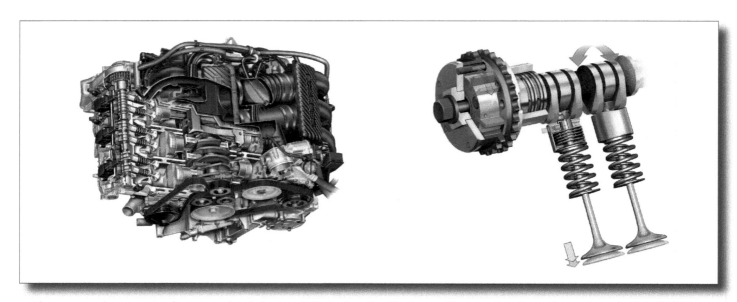

There was also a revised engine, this latest unit featuring the Variocam Plus mechanism, shown here in detail. With a familiar compression ratio of 11.3:1, the flat-six delivered a healthy 320bhp DIN.

The strict Carrera Cabriolet, complete with 18-inch 'Carrera' alloys.

The drophead version of the Carrera 4 for 2002.

NA machines joining the line-up for the 2002 season, the 911 range was essentially complete once again.

The new Carreras

For 2002, the regular normally-aspirated 911 range was given a new 3.6-litre engine, now matching the displacement of the turbocharged six and the limited run GT3. Actually, the 3.6-litre capacity was achieved by quite a different route, the older engines opting for a familiar 100 x 76.4mm bore and stroke (as used in the 964s and 993s, but water-cooled),

whilst the latest 996 Carreras went for a 96 x 82.8mm combination, giving 3596cc instead of 3600cc. This increase in capacity gave the new Carreras a useful boost in power and torque, now up to 320bhp DIN (315 SAE nett) and 273lbft, respectively.

The new engine was not only more powerful, but smoother and cleaner, too, as well as more frugal (officially 25.5mpg on average), all thanks to the latest Variocam technology. The version of Variocam used on the 3.4-litre engines was quite clever, employing tension in the timing chain

to adjust the intake camshaft position. This relatively simple method had limited movement, however. For the 2002 Carreras, Variocam Plus was introduced, as on the Turbo, allowing up to 40 degrees of adjustment.

To quote the publicity material: "With Variocam technology, the engine management system can modify the timing on the intake valves based on engine speed and load. Exclusively developed and patented by Porsche, Variocam uses a rotary vane adjuster on the intake camshaft to modify the point at which the intake valves open and close. As well as enhancing power and torque, the system offers smoother performance, improved fuel economy and lower exhaust emissions.

"Essentially, Variocam offers two engines in one, seamlessly adapting to changing performance requirements. At low engine speeds, idling is improved while emissions and fuel consumption are reduced. At medium revs, the system maximizes torque for more immediate acceleration. In the upper rev band, timing is adjusted for maximum outright performance."

It's fair to say that virtually everything was new for the M96/03 engine. The crankcase was modified for the first time, playing host to a new crank carrier and crankshaft, the latter with larger big-end bearings. The pistons, rings and connecting rods were also revised, along with the heads, camshafts, valves, air filter housing, air mass sensor, ignition components, the DME (ME 7.8) unit, and the exhaust system. Detail changes were applied to the oil pump, oil separator, cooling hoses, and the auxiliary belt drive tensioner as well.

The transmissions were also updated, with the G96/00 becoming the G96/01 on the strict Carrera, and the G96/31 replacing the G96/30 on the manual C4. There was also a new clutch pressure plate and release bearing, and gear selector cable. The Tiptronic gearbox, in particular, was heavily modified, with the A96/00 becoming the A96/10 and the A96/30 being replaced by the A96/35. The automatic also received a new gear selector cable,

From the front, it was impossible to tell the difference between a regular Carrera and its four-wheel drive stablemate (the Targa looked the same, too, but the lack of metalwork at the top of the windscreen was a giveaway if one could see that area). This coupé is a C4, however.

The Carrera range received yet another revised instrument cluster for 2002, basically mirroring that of the Turbo, with new calibrations on the tachometer.

The latest Carrera interior, as seen here nestling in a Speed Yellow Cabriolet.

along with a new gearknob and a revised selector mechanism. The Cardan shaft transmitting drive to the front on the C4 was modified, and the rear driveshafts uprated on all cars. Despite all these transmission changes, however, all ratios were carried over.

The latest styling was much easier to spot, though, with a new bumper front and rear, and Turbo-style headlights the most obvious feature. Less obvious was additional reinforcement in the roof and inner sill area, as well as the inner wheelwell panels. The bumpers were stronger as well as more stylish, with redesigned tailpipes (resembling a flattened oval shape) poking out at the back. This body strengthening added 25kg (55lb)

Both photos: The C4S was another blast from the past, with its Turbo-style bodywork. Note the unique badge, with 'Carrera 4' in silver, and the 'S' in grey at the end.

to the car's kerb weight, but it kept the 911 well ahead of the world's safety requirements.

The windscreen and screen trim was changed at the same time, as was the rear glass and trim on the coupé. The Cabriolet gained a new top covering and, at last, a glass rear window (complete with a heater element), along with new wiring and hydraulics that allowed the hood to operate whilst on the move. All cars were given new front lid and door locks (the luggage compartment lock mechanism being modified to incorporate an entrapment release), and the fuel tank and fuel pump were also revised. Finally, the 'Carrera' and 'Carrera 4' badges were moved further down on the back panel.

The M413, M414, XRB and XRL optional alloys continued, augmented by a new 18-inch five-spoke 'Carrera' rim (M411). At the same time, the M396 and M399 wheels were replaced by a new 17-inch ten-spoke design. Apart from the C4S, which inherited the M415 rims from the Turbo, the pressure cast M392 'Carrera II' rim (7J front, 9J rear) was standard fare for all the other NA 911s, shod with the same 205/50 and 255/40 ZR-rated rubber as before.

Beyond the wheels, the front and rear crossmembers were revised, the Bilstein shock absorbers were recalibrated (Bilsteins were used for both the standard and M030 suspension, just stiffer for the latter), the spring rates changed, the front wheel carriers and wheel bearings were uprated, and the rear track control arms modified. In addition, the PAS and brake fluid reservoirs received attention, along with most of the brake lines.

Moving inside, the fascia was changed to incorporate a glovebox, and the centre console modified to house a proper cupholder just below the reshaped air vents. This was fitted as standard on all cars, as was a three-spoke steering and a trip computer, the latter leading to a new layout in the digital sections of the gauges (as per the Turbo). The headlight and console-mounted switches were given a matt rather than gloss black finish, as

The C4S at speed ...

were the column stalks and cigarette lighter, answering complaints that the original items looked rather cheap for a high quality sports car.

The tunnel console also looked less plasticky, the rooflining (now Alcantara) and interior light were improved, and there were new seltbelt pretensioners and load limiters for enhanced safety; seatbelts were available in red, yellow or blue, in addition to the traditional black.

The new C4S and Targa variants
The Carrera 4S followed the same format as its earlier namesake, being

Both photos: The Targa made a welcome return to the line-up, coming with a lifting tailgate in 996 form. This was actually something Butzi Porsche had requested for the original 911, but the proposal was rejected in the early 1960s. Note the traditional 'Targa' badge (in black), and the different rear pillar and side window shapes.

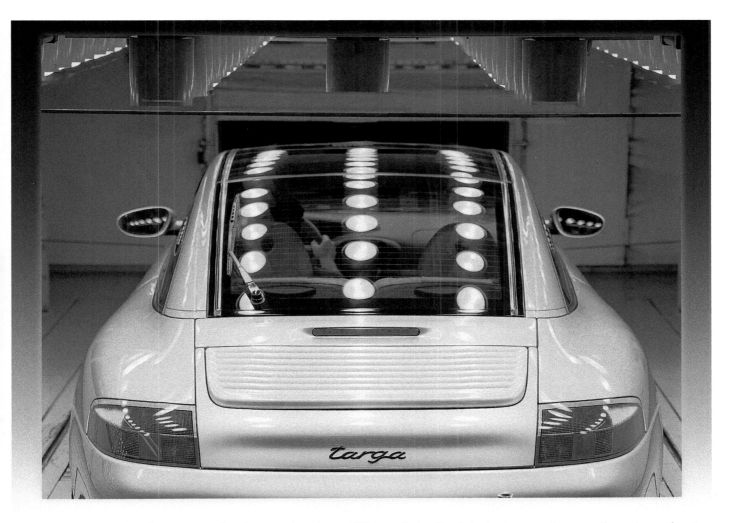

An interesting shot of a Targa in the climatic chamber at Weissach, testing interior temperatures under extreme heat.

a Carrera 4 with a Turbo-style body, its uprated suspension and braking system, its wheel and tyre combination (with 17mm/0.67in. wheel spacers on both sides and a '4S' logo in the wheel centres), and the turbocharged car's full leather interior.

There were several unique features for the C4S, introduced at €87,000, such as a heavy reflective band between the rear lights, rather like the older 911s, and a glassfibre engine cover to match up with it (this material was chosen to reduce tooling costs more than anything else). The regular Carrera rear spoiler was used, with the 'Carrera 4S' badge located in the same place as earlier 996 models. One will notice that there was no

air intake aft of the doors, but the C4S did get Litronic lights, a rain sensing windscreen, sports exhaust system, and 'Carrera 4S' script on the treadplates, aping that on the tail.

While the C4S weighed 65kg (143lb) more than the strict Carrera 4 coupé, at 1415kg (3113lb), the new Targa, at spot-on 1500kg (3300lb) actually weighed 10kg (22lb) less than the rear-wheel drive drophead.

The Targa also followed an established format, with a full-length glass roof and sharper rear side window graphics. Again, the glass retracted gracefully to sit inside the rear window, but the new Targa had a rear hatch. Supported by two gas struts, the rear window lifted

up to give a far more practical load carrying arrangement, although, when fitted, a unique rear wiper was called for, mounted directly on the glass. Otherwise, apart from the black 'Targa' badge on the tail and the extra switches on the centre console (to operate the roof and its roller blind), it was much the same as the regular Carrera.

News from Germany
New leather, carbon and wood trim packages were introduced to augment the existing ones, while the optional DSP amplifier was superceded by a Bose unit coming with subwoofers and new dash-mounted speakers (the grilles being in black or interior

trim colour). The Bose stereo was standard on the Turbo, and available as an option on the other 911s, duly replacing the other audio system upgrades on the options list, while a radio/CD unit and the CDC-3 CD changer (M692) was optional for all cars.

For 2002, Turbo buyers were given the option of greater power output, the X50 option upgrading the M96/70 engine into the M96/70E unit. A series of tweaks released 30 more horses, and took maximum torque output up to 457lbft. In order to handle the additional power, an uprated clutch plate was included in the price.

And for the race enthusiast, there was the 'Cup Aerokit II' which transformed the regular Carrera into a 2003 GT3 lookalike. The kit consisted of side skirts, a deeper front bumper with more aggressive air intake styling, and a rear wing sat atop a base. As before, it was possible to buy the rocker panel extensions separately, enabling the owner to match them with the tamer 'Carrera' (XAG) rear spoiler.

A total of 7660 911s were sold in Germany in 2001 – almost a 10 per cent improvement on 2000, and 878 units up on 1999 figures. However, while Porsche's links with Valmet grew stronger, production in Germany was seriously disturbed by a strike during the spring of 2002. It made the ZDF news on a regular basis, often as the top story. Fortunately, the dispute was settled, and 2002 would ultimately be a bumper year for the Stuttgart concern.

Above & opposite: Two pieces of German advertising from 2002.

Standard coachwork colours (2002)
Black, Carrara White, Guards Red, and Speed Yellow.

Metallic coachwork colours (2002)
Basalt Black Metallic, Arctic Silver Metallic, Seal Grey Metallic, Orient Red Metallic, Lapis Blue Metallic, Pearl Orange-Red (Zanzibar Red), Rainforest (Jungle) Green Metallic, and Meridian Metallic.

Special coachwork colours (2002)
Polar Silver Metallic, Slate Grey Metallic, Cobalt Blue Metallic, Midnight Blue Metallic, and Forest Green Metallic.

Cabriolet hood colours (2002)
Black, Graphite Grey, and Metropol Blue.

Trim colours & materials (2002)
Black, Graphite Grey, Metropol Blue, Nephrite or Savanna Beige vinyl, with Black, Graphite Grey, Metropol Blue, Nephrite or Savanna Beige leather as an option; special leathers included Natural Dark Grey, Boxster Red, Natural Brown or Cinnamon. Carpets came in Black, Graphite Grey, Natural Dark Grey, Boxster Red, Metropol Blue, Nephrite, Natural Brown, Cinnamon or Savanna Beige.

America's 2002 season

The US 911 range for 2002 included the rear-wheel drive Carrera in coupé and Cabriolet guises, the new Targa, the C4S coupé (which replaced the regular C4 coupé in the line-up), the C4 Cabriolet, the Turbo, and the Turbo-based GT2, the latter limited to 250 units for the States.

Prices started at $67,900 for the tin-top RR Carrera with manual transmission, and went all the way up to $179,900 for the new GT2. Most of the small increase over 2001 season sticker prices can be assigned to the use of a leather-wrapped three-spoke steering wheel for all models (with matching gearknob and handbrake trim), an immobilizer system (operated by a transponder key with a built-in lamp and a Porsche crest on it), and the standard onboard computer; as before, US cars had rubber buffers surrounding the rear number plate, but they were more stylish than earlier versions. As a matter of interest, it was

A Carrera Cabriolet with Exclusive interior trim.

Hier erfahren Sie mehr – Porsche Online: Telefon/Fax 01805 · 356 911 (EUR 0,12/min) oder www.porsche.com.

Offen? Geschlossen?
Sieht so aus,
als müßten Sie sich entscheiden.
Für beides.

Der neue 911 Targa.

almost possible to buy the cheapest Carrera and a normal $115,000 Turbo for the price of a GT2!

Stateside sales dropped slightly in 2002. All told, 9875 Boxsters were sold (2403 less than in 2001), but 911 sales were up a touch, to 11,443 units. The total sales figure for 2002 was 21,318 units – about 8 per cent down on the previous year.

The UK, Japan & Australia

The euro (€) was officially adopted as the EU's currency on the first day of 2002, although some countries had been pricing goods in euros from

continued page 168

An alternative interior with trim components selected from the Exclusive catalogue. The list of possibilities was almost endless ...

Below & opposite page: The Cup Aerokit II for the Carrera coupé. Note the NA sports exhaust tailpipes, with the slightly different C4S, Turbo and GT2 version at the top of the page. The other detail shot shows the alternative rear spoiler for the Carrera, listed alongside the one included in the original Cup body kit.

as early as 1999; Britain, however, continued to price things in sterling.

The revised Carrera coupé was listed at £55,950, with the Cabriolet commanding a £62,000 sticker price. Adding four-wheel drive bumped up the invoice by a reasonable £3700 on the coupé and £3750 on the drophead, while Tiptronic transmission added a premium of around £2000. The

Above: Optional rear spoiler for the Turbo, which usually came with a front apron piece that extended further forward, and had small vents below the main outer intakes.

Right & opposite page: American brochure for the face-lifted Carrera range.

The more things change...

168

The more things stay the same.

The best sports car under the sun.

Traditionalists would insist that the only true sports car is an open car. That the visceral pleasures of sun and wind and the music of the road are absolutely essential to the performance experience. Who are we to argue? Rather, we prefer to offer a thoroughbred 911 Carrera Cabriolet and an all-wheel drive Carrera 4 Cabriolet designed to heighten the pleasure of top-down driving in every way imaginable. The 911 Cabriolets effortlessly blend the primal rush of a potent 320 horsepower engine with the sophistication of a push button top, now featuring a heated glass rear window. In addition, they deliver handling prowess and agility that will inject life into every back road and coastal highway. All that's required of you is a free afternoon and a taste for adventure.

It's never easy to improve a 911, but we always do.

Maybe it's all those decades of racing heritage, but Porsche engineers never [...] that when you [...] catches [...] development [...]. In the [...] signed [...] signed front and rear fenders that reduce lift for improved high-speed stability and increase cooling air by 15%. The larger 3.6 liter engine now features VarioCam Plus, a valve timing system to optimize power and torque while reducing emissions and fuel consumption. The optional Tiptronic S gearbox comes from the 911 Turbo to accommodate the increased performance. The suspension has been retuned based on lessons learned from the race-bred GT-3. Even the alloy wheels have received attention, now lighter in weight by almost 10% for better handling.

Ready, come rain or come shine.

Targa isn't the German word for versatile, but maybe it should be. When the weather's fine, the new Targa's unique glass top slides open to deliver virtually all the open-air driving pleasure of the 911 Cabriolet. When the temperature drops or the weather turns threatening, the top closes to seal things up as snug and tight as a 911 Coupe. The large glass rear window can be used as a hatch to gain convenient access to the rear storage area. Motoring enclosed or alfresco, the cockpit is equally comfortable and accommodating. Like all 2002 911 models, the Targa features a redesigned instrument panel, improved amenities such as a lockable, lighted glove box, new cup holders and the incredible sonic realism of an available 12-speaker Bose® sound system.

Inspired by Velcro®.

The Carrera 4S is all about handling, about agility, precision and confidence-inspiring control when the road snakes every which way but straight. An advanced, full-time all-wheel drive system automatically directs the power to the wheels with the best grip. A quartet of red four-piston fixed calipers and larger 13" ventilated brake disks from the 911 Turbo, make the Carrera 4S ideally suited for winding mountain roads. But that's not all. The Porsche Stability Management (PSM) system further balances the performance of the Carrera 4S in a way that smoothes and complements your driving skills. A wider track and wider stance enhance stability and combine with the sophisticated all-wheel drive system to deliver uncompromised performance regardless of the weather, the road or the conditions. Prepare to be amazed.

169

The GT2 taking centre stage on the Porsche stand at the 2001 San Francisco Motor Show, held in November. (Courtesy Ken Hoyle)

Turbo was priced at £87,250, with the GT2 version coming in at £114,900. Meanwhile, the new Targa was introduced at £61,000, and the C4S just £1260 more.

Autocar tried the new entry-level Carrera for size, and found: "The engine is constantly poised to let you take its rev needle up to the red zone whenever you feel inclined. This truly is a great engine: One that basks in its heritage and by every objective measure improves on its predecessor. It also demolishes every air-cooled normally-aspirated lump the company has ever made.

"More worrying for rival car makers, Porsche has infused the chassis with an equal dose of brilliance. To experience it working over a road, filtering out the unnecessary, passing on the necessary, is to experience one of motoring's finer offerings. As before, control is the key. From small to massive speeds, the Porsche's body movements are resolutely kept in check, leaving the driver to savour a steering rack of rare brilliance.

Press image of the 2002 Turbo for the US market.

"And it's fun. Fun in a way that lets the driver exploit that list of abilities, and revel in the fact that Porsche continues to manage the impossible; namely, disguise the fact that this car's engine is in entirely the wrong place. So you get all the traction benefits and none of the horror stories of the old car. Sure, a silly entry speed and a trailing throttle will still create an interesting angle of approach, but leave the stability and traction control on and even that's taken care of. Grip, wet or dry, is ample and the optional [sport] seats are more than capable of coping with the forces.

"It's a dangerous sport calling such expensive machinery a bargain, but no other word does the new 911 justice. It's a stunner."

Official figures quoted a top speed of 178mph (285kph) and a 0-60 time of five seconds dead. The *Autocar* test recorded 177mph (283kph) and 4.6 seconds for these most recognized of automotive yardsticks, putting the car in touch with cars like the Aston Martin DB7, the Honda NSX, and even the Ferrari 360 Modena in terms of real world performance.

Meanwhile, Jason Barlow tried the GT2 for *GQ Magazine*, noting: "As with every 911, the GT2 is a master-class in feel and poise. Provided you know what you're doing, half an hour on a good road is an almost transcendental experience. So many cars nowadays feel synthetic, but the GT2 is primal and earthy, devoted to keeping it real. It's also faultlessly screwed together,

Cover of the Japanese 'Selection' catalogue for the 2002 season.

A Carrera Cabriolet at the San Francisco event. (Courtesy Ken Hoyle)

The Cabriolet and Targa at the 2001 Tokyo Show, held that year from 26 October to 7 November.

not something you can take for granted, even at this price level."

There was little to write home about in Japan, although sales kept rising, and the 911 range was very extensive, as can be seen from the table below.

In Australia, the cheapest car in the 2002 Porsche line-up was the 2.7-litre Boxster, which cost $108,900. Carrera prices started at $186,000, with the Turbo listed at $306,000, and the GT2 now available at $399,000.

2002 competition review

The FIA GT Championship was the realm of the Chrysler Viper and Ferrari 550 Maranello, although the Lister Storm provided some excellent competition. 911 drivers were strong in the N-GT Class, with Stephane Ortelli coming through to take the driver's title by a convincing margin,

Japanese price list: 2002 MY		
	Manual	**Tiptronic**
Carrera coupé	9,900,000 yen	10,700,000 yen
Carrera Cabriolet	11,500,000 yen	12,300,000 yen
C4 coupé	10,900,000 yen	11,700,000 yen
C4 Cabriolet	12,500,000 yen	13,300,000 yen
911 Targa	11,100,000 yen	11,900,000 yen
Carrera 4S	11,700,000 yen	12,500,000 yen
911 Turbo	16,800,000 yen	17,600,000 yen
911 GT2	23,440,000 yen	–

after Ferrari's domination fizzled out early in the season; Ortelli also won the 2002 Supercup.

Audi won again at Le Mans, but the Racer's Group GT3RS of Timo Bernhard, Lucas Luhr and Kevin Buckler came in 16th to take GT honours. Audi also took the increasingly important ALMS title, although Lucas Luhr and Sascha Maassen notched up a Class win with the Alex Job Racing 911 to give Porsche the GT crown by a staggering margin. Kevin Buckler came third in the GT title chase, with Jorg Bergmeister fourth, and Timo Bernhard fifth. In the Grand-Am series, Porsche beat Ferrari in the GT title chase, and came second in the GTS category (Saleen took the honours in that Class).

As well as representation in the Carrera Cup Japan, there was still a strong 911 field in the GT300 category of the JGTC but, once again, winning drivers were equipped with Japanese machinery – this time the Toyota MR-S (better known as the MR2 in export markets) stole the glory.

The 2003 model year

The Boxster was given a major face-lift at this time, but there was also a brand new Porsche launched for 2003 – the Cayenne. Developed jointly with Volkswagen (VW had its own version called the Touareg), the Cayenne was the sporting SUV that had been in the pipeline for quite some time.

The Cayenne was basically a response to market trends, particularly in America and Japan. The SUV may be a fast-selling fashion statement, but few are fun to drive, so the brief given to Porsche engineers was to make a vehicle with all the practical and luxury elements one associates with the premium 4x4 breed, endow it with superb off-road capability, and even better performance on the road. As the factory stated: "Porsche is known for outstanding performance, agile handling, excellent driving dynamics and superior safety. Now, Porsche is carrying over this philosophy into the segment of sport utility vehicles – without neglecting the demand for outstanding off-road capability."

In reality, few expensive 4x4s are ever driven off-road (image seems to be more important), but four-wheel drive does at least occasionally prove useful in the winter in colder areas. For those who did wander off the beaten track, electronics were used to apportion drive to the wheels with most traction (as well as control ride height and suspension settings), and the 4WD system was definitely able to handle almost any obstacle put before it.

Porsche's reputation for high-performance was upheld with a pair of 4.5-litre V8 engines – a normally-aspirated 340bhp S version, and one

Japanese advertising from early 2002 showing a 911 Cabriolet treated to a number of options from the Exclusive catalogue.

ニュー911に乗るか、
私だけのニュー911に乗るか。

テーラーメイドのスーツを仕立てるように。
その走りとフォルムを磨きぬいたニュー911を、
より個性あふれる一台へと進化させていく歓びがある。
"エクスクルーシブ"—それはポルシェを愉しみつくす最高の方法。
ステアリングを握る前から、物語はもう走りはじめているのだ。
超えてゆく人生に——ポルシェ。

PORSCHE

Sears Point in the spring of 2002, with a 996 in the scrutineering bay prior to an ALMS race.

A 370bhp GT3 Cup model prepared to promote the 2002 Porsche Carrera Cup Japan. The Supercup cars were given the modified front mask of their roadgoing counterparts for the 2002 season, as well as a subtle boost in power, taking the peak up to 380bhp.

with twin-turbos, taking power up to 450bhp and the top speed to a heady 165mph (264kph). Only the Tiptronic transmission was offered and body control was largely down to electronic wizardry, but early road tests offered few complaints. The engineers had obviously succeeded in meeting all the required targets.

Built in a new factory in Leipzig, a 247bhp V6-engined Cayenne was added for the 2004 season, coming with the option of a manual gearbox.

The 2003 911 range
Changes were few for 2003, limited to a revised shift lever bracket on manual cars, new shock absorbers for the majority of NA models, a new steering angle sensor, a modified handbrake lever mechanism, new gearknobs, and a different accelerator pedal unit. In addition, the Turbo gained new exhaust heat protection panels, and the audio system was fully overhauled and updated for all cars.

A radio/CD (CDR-23) unit became standard across the board, the Turbo having 12 speakers, while the C4S got ten. The Bose High End Sound Package fitted to the Turbo and the Hi-Fi Sound system of the Carrera 4S were optional on lesser 911s, while a new CDC-4 autochanger was optional for all models, and this could be linked to the latest fibre optic stereo equipment, called MOST (standing for Media Oriented Systems Transport), for the ultimate in sound quality.

A new 18-inch five-spoke 'Sport Techno' (XRC) rim was added to the optional alloy wheel listing, requiring a steel valve, but available for all 911s. Meanwhile, the X51 option brought with it more power for the NA Carreras, with various modifications (including different intake manifolds and camshafts, and a completely new exhaust system) boosting power to 345bhp DIN at 6800rpm. Torque was unchanged at 273lbft, but maximum output was developed at 4800 instead of 4250rpm with the engine in uprated guise.

At the end of 2002, no fewer than 8937 911s were sold in Germany. In fact, it was a bumper year for the evergreen Porsche, with a record production figure posted for the RR model. So, was the 911 still a star attraction? Most certainly, and

Standard coachwork colours (2003)
Black, Carrara White, Guards Red, and Speed Yellow.

Metallic coachwork colours (2003)
Basalt Black Metallic, Arctic Silver Metallic, Seal Grey Metallic, Orient Red Metallic, Lapis Blue Metallic, Midnight Blue Metallic, Lagoon Green (Dark Teal) Metallic, and Meridian Metallic.

Cabriolet Hood Colours (2003)
Black, Graphite Grey, and Metropol Blue.

Trim colours & materials (2003)
Black, Graphite Grey, Metropol Blue, Nephrite or Savanna Beige vinyl, with Black, Graphite Grey, Metropol Blue, Nephrite or Savanna Beige leather as an option; special leathers included Natural Dark Grey, Boxster Red, Natural Brown or Cinnamon. Carpets came in Black, Graphite Grey, Natural Dark Grey, Boxster Red, Metropol Blue, Nephrite, Natural Brown, Cinnamon or Savanna Beige.

another new variant simply drove home the message ...

The new GT3
Making its debut alongside the production Carrera GT at the 2003 Geneva Show, the new GT3 was a welcome addition to the 911 line-up, especially in the States, where this most focused of rear-engined models was made available for the first time.

The body was basically that of the regular Carrera coupé with the 'Cup Aerokit II' aerodynamic appendages (including a new front bumper, side skirts and rear spoiler, the latter being adjustable with three preset positions). Although, as before, it was suitably strengthened, underbody spoilers were added around the suspension, and the discreet black 'GT3' badge on the tail hinted at something special lurking beneath the engine cover.

The engine's leading specifications were the same as those of the M96/76 which powered the earlier 996-based GT3, although the latest M96/79

version was legal in all countries. This was made possible due to the adoption of Variocam Plus and the latest Bosch engine management system (ME 7.8), but lightening the old unit's valvetrain, forged pistons and titanium conrods also allowed it to rev more freely. With the limiter set at the 8200rpm red-line, a maximum

The Cayenne, seen here with Wendelin Wiedeking (left) and Germany's Chancellor, Gerhard Schroeder, at the opening of the Leipzig plant.

of 381bhp DIN (375bhp SAE nett) was produced at 7400rpm, while 284lbft of torque was delivered at 5000rpm.

With regard to the six-speed transmission (Type G96/96), the first four gears were the same as those specified for the G96/90 gearbox used on the European GT3 (3.82, 2.15, 1.56 and 1.21 respectively), but

fifth became direct and sixth went to 0.85; the final-drive remained listed at 3.44:1, with the specification completed by a mechanical limited-slip differential and a dedicated transmission oil cooler. Optional gear ratio sets were available for those interested in racing.

Like its predecessor, the new GT3

boasted a lowered, uprated and fully adjustable suspension. There was a new braking system, though, with red six-pot calipers up front working on bigger, 350mm (13.8in) diameter discs, and four-pot calipers at the rear matched with 330mm (13.0in) rotors. ABS was standard, with ceramic brakes optional. There were also new

179

An interesting shot taken from the inside of the Targa. This picture clearly illustrates the light, airy feel afforded by the glass roof.

ten-spoke wheels with the 'GT3' logo in the wheel centres. The 8.5J x 18 and 11J x 18 rims were shod with Michelins made specifically for the GT3: These ZR-rated tyres (235/40 front, 295/30 rear) actually made a massive contribution to the GT3's high level of roadholding, with exceptional grip from the Pilot Sport N1 rubber.

Interior appointments were very much the same as before, with the latest improvements duly incorporated, although the regular three-point seatbelts had to be adopted as standard to comply with worldwide safety regulations. Despite the rear seats being deleted to help keep weight down to 1380kg (3036lb), the cockpit was actually very civilized, with a CD/radio and air conditioning classed as no cost options. The 'GT3' logo appeared on the 9400rpm tachometer, the floormats and rear bulkhead carpet, handbrake lever, and the treadplates.

Front and rear views of the new GT3, introduced at the 2003 Geneva Show.

Incidentally, a large-capacity 90-litre (19.8 Imperial gallon) fuel tank was fitted, as before, although rhd models had to make do with a regular tank to allow room for the spacesaver spare. With official fuel consumption quoted at 21.9mpg on average, this made an enormous difference to the car's touring range.

A Club Sport version was available for no extra charge, featuring a rollcage, a flame-retardant fabric seat covering, a six-point harness for the driver (supplied separately), a fire extinguisher and battery master cut-off switch. There was no limit on production for either variant.

Motor Trend tried one of the new models, and declared: "You know this is a different, more focused Carrera the instant you turn the key. The engine sounds edgier and cammier and revs quicker ... The intake and exhaust notes are richer and reedier and remind you of, well, how an old 911S would sound if it had 3.6-litres."

"Okay, the GT3 is still water-cooled. That aside, it'll ring your bell like no non-turbo 911 has for decades. The sharper, crisper, more driver-centric Carrera is here, and the 911 faithful will surely fight to get one."

Autocar asked the burning question: "So how much faster, precisely, is the new GT3 over the old? To get the clearest idea you must ignore the 0-60mph times of 4.8 seconds (old) versus 4.5 seconds (new). Check the 0-100mph runs – 10.9 seconds versus 9.3 – and the 30-70mph sprints (4.1 seconds versus 3.7). In both, the new car destroys its predecessor, and by doing so qualifies as a genuine supercar. Only 2mph has been added to the top speed, now 190mph."

It added: "The six-speed gearbox is as sweet as ever to use, and the way the clutch, differential and gearbox interact with each other remains one of the traits that distinguishes the 911: The drivetrain feels as strong as it is slick and is every bit as impressive as the engine."

In summary, *Autocar* loved the engine, brakes, steering (three turns lock-to-lock), gearchange and cabin quality, but was less enthusiastic about the very hard ride and the way it felt "nervous over bumpy B-roads."

However, whilst "not as good an all-rounder as the Turbo," it was declared better than the GT2 and summed up as "one of the, if not the, most exciting handlers this magazine has ever tested."

American news

The war in Iraq helped push up petrol prices to record levels in the States. 2003 Porsche sales were up, too, however, largely thanks to the Cayenne, as 911 sales fell slightly (the 911 line-up and leading specifications were unchanged from the previous season), and those recorded for the Boxster were 38 per cent down on the previous year.

Meanwhile, Frederick J. Schwab, who'd headed the PCNA operation for more than a decade, had stepped down from office on 1 March 2003, shortly after the Cayenne's US debut at the Detroit Show. Schwab handed the reins to Peter Schwarzenbauer after a fourth successive year of record sales for the 911.

The 911 was popular with members of the press, too. *Motor Trend* had a C4S in its long-term test fleet, and observed: "Leave it to Porsche to create a little piece of heaven and call it the Carrera 4S. The updated 3.6-litre boxer engine is rich in power over the entire rev band, and feedback – through the steering, throttle, and shift lever – is spot on. We're having trouble getting used to the excessive engine clatter at cold start-up, but the exhaust's song at full throttle reminds us that this was indeed engineered by people who are in love with automobiles ... This is a perfectly useable daily driver that masks a very effective supercar."

Car & Driver put the C4 Cabriolet up against the Cadillac XLR, Jaguar XK8, Lexus SC430 and Mercedes-Benz SL500 in a drophead shoot-out. All cars had automatic transmission to even up the playing field, and it was noted: "The Porsche's brakes are great, as usual. Steering feel is excellent. The tranny is the best of the bunch with full manual control. A very good driver's tool."

Indeed, everyone seemed to love the 911's performance and handling, but the price was thought to be on the high side, and the interior was said to be in need of a long overdue a face-lift. Ultimately, it was concluded: "Regardless of the price, it provides a unique and endlessly joyful driving experience." This was not enough, however, and the 911 had to settle for second place in the contest, trailing its Stuttgart rival on 183 points to the SL's 200.

At the heart of any Porsche is always its engine, only more so in the case of the GT3. This is the M96/79 power unit in all its glory.

The G96/96 six-speed transmission used in the GT3.

Interior of the regular GT3.

The right-hookers (rhd)

The 2002 British Motor Show was held at the NEC from 22 October to 3 November. Although the Cayenne took centre stage, introduced at £44,530 (or £68,970 in turbocharged guise), the revised Boxsters also made quite an impression. At this time, the 911 line-up ranged in price from £56,450 to £116,000, by the way – slightly up on last season. The new GT3 was introduced at £72,750, available with manual transmission only.

In the other major rhd markets, Japan and Australia, prices and leading specifications were carried over from the 2002 season, although November 2002 saw the Turbo 'High Performance Limited Edition' added in the Land of the Rising Sun (20 units, priced at 21,000,000 yen apiece, and similar to the 30 produced a year earlier), and then the GT3 models – the basic GT3 coupé introduced at around 14,000,000 yen.

Incidentally, Japan was officially in recession during the first years of the new century, although it was hard to believe for an Englishman living there. Doubtless there were still queues lining up to buy the 612bhp Carrera GT when it at last went on sale in April 2003, especially when people learnt that production (at the Leipzig factory, incidentally) was to be restricted to 1000 cars over three years! Whatever, the government declared that things were improving, and a full recovery had been announced by 2004.

Racing update

The FIA GT Championship was dominated by Ferrari in the GT Class, although Porsche pilots Stephane Ortelli and Marc Lieb were declared winners of the N-GT category, which turned out to be a straight fight between the Stuttgart and Modena rivals.

Still in Europe, Bentley won Le Mans, marking the return of a great marque, although some pointed out that the lack of any real competition made it rather a hollow victory. Whatever – a win is a win, and that's the bottom line. Meanwhile, Lucas Luhr and Sascha Maassen teamed up with Emmanuel Pollard to take their GT3RS to a creditable 14th and a Class victory in the GT category.

continued page 190

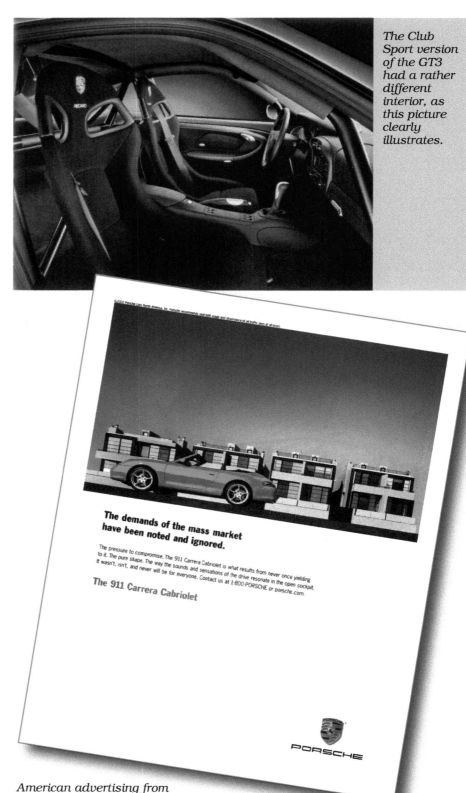

The Club Sport version of the GT3 had a rather different interior, as this picture clearly illustrates.

The demands of the mass market have been noted and ignored.

The pressure to compromise. The 911 Carrera Cabriolet is what results from never once yielding to it. The pure shape. The way the sounds and sensations of the drive resonate in the open cockpit. It wasn't, isn't, and never will be for everyone. Contact us at 1-800-PORSCHE or porsche.com.

The 911 Carrera Cabriolet

PORSCHE

American advertising from spring 2003.

A Targa at speed with roof retracted.

Exterior and interior of the 2003 MY Carrera coupé for the US market.

The 2003 model year Carrera 4S in US trim.

Stunning picture of the Federal GT2.

The Carrera Cabriolet for the North American 2003 season.

The Alex Job Racing 911 that won its Class at Le Mans.

The Racer's Group GT3RS at Le Mans. This equipe had already won at Daytona earlier in the year.

The Team Taisan Advan 911 captured on film just as darkness fell at Le Mans.

Pierre Kaffer in action in the 2003 Porsche Supercup.

Frank Stippler won the 2003 Supercup, whilst in the US-based ALMS series, Bentley's close cousin, Audi, won the title once again. In the GT category, Porsche drivers Lucas Luhr and Sascha Maassen emerged victorious at the end of the season, winning with the Alex Job Racing 911 as they had in 2002. In the Rolex-sponsored Grand-Am series, Ferrari beat Porsche by the narrowest of margins in the GT Class, and third was the best the German manufacturer could muster in the GTS grouping.

There were still no Porsches in the prestigious GT500 category of the JGTC, but plenty of GT3Rs running in GT300. Despite this, the Class fell to a Japanese car driver, although Shinichi Yamaji and Kazuyuki Nishizawa came joint-second in the 2003 title chase.

The Carrera 4S and Turbo Cabriolets

When the 2003 Frankfurt Show opened its doors to the public on September 13, Porsche fans headed straight for Hall 5. In addition to some old favourites, stand B06 featured the V6-powered Cayenne, the Carrera 4S Cabriolet, the Turbo Cabriolet, and the wonderful GT3RS (based on the recently-revived GT3, and now available in all markets, unlike the first version). There was also a 40th anniversary 911 coupé to commemorate four decades of the evergreen, rear-engined Porsche.

Official pictures of the C4S Cabriolet were released some time before the Frankfurt Show, and deposits were already being taken during the early part of the summer. It basically followed the same format established with the C4S coupé, with the Turbo body and chassis combined with NA Carrera 4 running gear, and had the same distinguishing details as its tin-top cousin, such as a lack of air intakes just aft of the doors and the reflective band between the rear lights.

Weighing in at 1610kg (3542lb), the C4S Cabriolet was 60kg (132lb) heavier than the regular C4 Cabriolet. Some of this was due to additional strengthening added in the B-post area, executed in DP600 high-tensile steel. This reinforcement was deemed necessary to retain rigidity in the more powerful Turbo Cabriolet, but it was shared with the normally-aspirated car for ease of manufacture. The Turbo Cabriolet was 60kg (132lb) heavier than the C4S Cabriolet, incidentally, and an aluminium hardtop was included in the price of both in most markets.

The Turbo Cabriolet was also basically the same as its closed-bodied counterpart. One feature, however, was unique to this model from an open-bodied point of view – the third brake light was mounted on the rear spoiler instead of the hood cover. This was due to adoption of the Turbo's two-piece rear wing, but instead of making do with the regular tonneau cover section with its integral high-mount brake light (as fitted to all other drophead 911s), a new panel was made exclusively for the new turbocharged model.

The GT3RS

Announced on 1 July 2003, sales of the latest 911 to wear the legendary Rennsport insignia did not start until October. Sales of more than 200 units were needed to comply with the FIA's GT homologation regulations, so the car was fully road legal in most countries, with the notable exception of North America.

The RS was essentially a GT3 Club Sport that had been on a strict diet. Indeed, the RS was 50kg (110lb) lighter than a GT3 CS, improving on the former's power-to-weight ratio by as much as 4 per cent, despite the GT3RS officially having the same power and torque as the strict GT3. The RS's 0-60 time was listed in

ALMS racers in downtown San Jose promoting the September meeting at Laguna Seca. Johnny Mowlem's 911 GT3RS can be seen next to Jan Magnussen's Ferrari. Mowlem came 14th in the race. (Courtesy Ken Hoyle)

Final preparation for the GT3RSs of Alex Job Racing. (Courtesy Ken Hoyle)

the catalogue as 4.4 seconds, with a top speed of 191mph (306kph) – fractionally better than the regular GT3. On the race track, of course, it's fractions of a second that make all the difference between winning and losing ...

At first glance, it was easy to dismiss the RS as a normal GT3, or even a Carrera with the 'Cup II'

body kit; closer inspection revealed a fixed carbonfibre rear wing (supplied separately in some countries for legal reasons – these markets having a regular GT3 spoiler for road use), and a different intake to increase airflow to the engine bay. The front lid and mirrors were also carbonfibre, a plastic rear screen replaced the normal glass one, and even the front

Front and rear views of the new Turbo Cabriolet.

badge was a sticker to save weight, as was the 'GT3 RS' example on the tail. There was also a slit ahead of the front lid, aping that of the GT2 and Carrera Cup racers.

Finished in Carrara White only, the RS was available with nostalgic red or blue 'GT3 RS' decals for the side of the car, the coloured band extending to the front and rear bumpers. Wheels and tyres were carried over (in fact, apart from a few racing parts for the suspension, all running gear was similar to that of the regular GT3), but the wheel centres were red or blue, painted to match the optional stickers, and came with a polished rim to serve as a further reminder of the earliest 911 RS models.

Inside, a rollcage was standard (either the black Club Sport version or an optional lightweight cage in white), and three dials were fitted for heating and ventilation (although air conditioning was available for those in warmer climes). The door speakers were deleted, as was the glovebox and some of the soundproofing, and the steering wheel, gearlever gaiter and handbrake boot were trimmed

Seine Performance mag außergewöhnlich sein. Und doch gibt es Tage, an denen Sie mit jedem anderen Auto schneller zu Hause wären.

Das neue 911 Carrera 4S Cabriolet.

PORSCHE

Domestic advertising for the new Carrera 4S Cabriolet. Whilst the press launch was held in the picturesque Austrian Alps, this promotional shot was taken in the States.

Luxurious interior of the drophead version of the Turbo.

A Turbo Carbriolet with its hood in place.

in Alcantara, with either red or blue stitching to match the wheels and side decals. Club Sport seats were adopted, coming with either red or blue seatbelts.

Other 2004 MY news

To commemorate the 40th anniversary of the 911, a special car – limited to 1963 units worldwide – was announced, based on the regular Carrera coupé. The '40 Jahre' celebration model came with a 345bhp engine (the X51 option) and a manual transmission, the latter dictated by the uprated power-unit, which was not available with the Tiptronic S gearbox. The M030 suspension was combined with PSM to keep everything in check.

Finished in GT Silver Metallic, this 181mph (290kph) model featured a Turbo-style front mask with Litronic headlights (complete with washers), side skirts, and polished 18-inch 'Carrera' wheels. Around the back, it had special badging and chrome tailpipes, while inside, the numbered badge used on the 'Millennium Special' was revived, and the heated seats were trimmed in Natural Grey leather.

The '40 Jahre' 911 carried a sticker price of €95,616, by the way. To put that into perspective, in Germany, and most of Europe for that matter, the basic Carrera was priced at €74,504 at this time, the drophead version being €84,480, the Turbo €128,676, and the new Turbo Cabriolet introduced at €138,652 (€38,860 more than the C4S Cabriolet). The regular GT3 was €102,112, against €120,788 for the GT3RS, and €184,674 for the turbocharged GT2.

The GT2 was an expensive piece of machinery, but for 2004 it was given an even more powerful engine. Changes to the ECU, pistons, rings and cylinder liners gave birth to the M96/70SL unit, which delivered 483bhp at 5700rpm, and 462lbft of torque at 3500rpm. As a result, the car's top speed increased very slightly, but few would ever experience the giddy heights of the GT2's performance envelope. Other changes for the GT2 included a modified braking system (the ABS was now version 5.7, as per the other 911s), and a stronger, lighter rear spoiler was adopted for the Club Sport version.

A body kit became available for the C4S (code XAH), which looked just like the Turbo one (XAF). It was now possible to have the air intakes in the Turbo and C4S front bumper painted in body colour, and all cars could have the rear model designation badge colour-keyed if the owner wished.

The optional M413 and M414 Turbo Look rims were deleted at the end of the 2003 season, and the M415

Various shots of Michihiko Higashida's GT3RS at Nobel in Chiba (formally known as K3 Works).

Standard coachwork colours (2004)
Black, Carrara White, Guards Red, and Speed Yellow.

Metallic coachwork colours (2004)
Basalt Black Metallic, Arctic Silver Metallic, Atlas Grey Metallic, Seal Grey Metallic, Carmona Red Metallic, Lapis Blue Metallic, Midnight Blue Metallic, and Lagoon Green (Dark Teal) Metallic.

Special coachwork colours (2004)
Polar Silver Metallic, Slate Grey Metallic, Meridan Metallic, Cobalt Blue Metallic, and Forest Green Metallic.

Cabriolet hood colours (2004)
Black, Graphite Grey, and Metropol Blue.

Trim colours & materials (2004)
Black, Graphite Grey, Metropol Blue or Savanna Beige vinyl, with Black, Graphite Grey, Metropol Blue or Savanna Beige leather as an option; special leathers included Natural Dark Grey, Boxster Red, Natural Brown or Cinnamon. Carpets came in Black, Graphite Grey, Natural Dark Grey, Boxster Red, Metropol Blue, Natural Brown, Cinnamon or Savanna Beige.

Tasteful German advertising for the '40 Jahre' celebration model.

Hier erfahren Sie alles über den 911 – Porsche Online: Telefon 01805 356 - 911, Fax - 912 (EUR 0,12/min) oder www.porsche.com.

Einer der ganz wenigen Serienhelden, die mit dem Alter immer besser werden.

Das 911 Jubiläumsmodell.

Mehr über die ersten 40 Jahre 911 erfahren Sie unter www.porsche.com.

PORSCHE

wheel had taken on the Turbo Look II moniker by this time. Including the latter, there were now five alloy wheel options for the 911s, in addition to standard rims.

Manual rear-wheel drive Carreras were given the option of a traditional mechanical limited-slip differential (M220) on cars with 18-inch wheels, and there was a Sport gearshift, reducing strokes between the gears by as much as 35 per cent (option code XCZ). In addition, a thicker rimmed three-spoke steering wheel became available for the first time.

Export market review
In the States, the 911 range consisted of ten basic cars: The Carrera coupé ($68,600); the Targa ($76,000); Carrera Cabriolet ($78,400); C4S coupé ($83,400); C4 Cabriolet ($84,000); C4S Cabriolet ($93,200); the GT3 ($99,900); the Turbo coupé ($118,400); Turbo Cabriolet ($128,200), and the flagship GT2 model ($191,700). Add in the option

continued page 200

Australian price list: 2004 MY	Manual	Tiptronic
Carrera coupé	$187,600	$195,600
Carrera Cabriolet	$203,700	$211,700
911 Targa	$205,400	$213,400
Carrera 4S	$225,300	$233,300
911 GT3	$241,500	–
911 Turbo	$308,900	$316,900

Interior and tail of the '40 Jahre' model.

A 2004 model year Carrera 4 coupé pictured in the Weissenhof area of Stuttgart.

The 2004 Turbo for the American market.

A couple of artistic shots showing the US-spec Targa for the 2004 season.

Cover of the PCNA 2004 range brochure, with the Carrera GT above a Boxster, Cayenne and 911.

chin spoiler scraped on every speed bump and even the most modestly sloped driveways. Too much hassle for something that is obviously not a track car. A cruiser should be easier in the city.

"In the end, this one left me cold, a mixed up kid – half racer/half roller with too much of the edge buffed off, but hardly soft or easy. The Carrera 4S Cabriolet seems optimized for posing, yet safe enough to hand over to your mom for her Sunday drive. It's a great car for someone who wants the Porsche image and performance without any of the quirkiness or purist appeal a true Porschephile savours."

Paul Frere was also disappointed with the "showy" demeanour of the C4S models, which were simply too heavy compared to the narrow-bodied cars. Nevertheless, the 911 was declared top premium sports car in the 2004 JD Power Survey, whilst British enthusiasts celebrated the completion of the 911 line-up, with the £70,135 C4S Cabriolet proving popular amongst newer fans of the marque. PCGB sold 2904 911s in 2003, along with 3218 Boxsters and around 1800 Cayennes.

In Australia, sales were slow but steady, as always. The 2004 model year line-up, at least at the start of the season, was as per the table on page 196.

Most prices were carried over in Japan for the 2004 season, although the C4S coupé was a touch more expensive (starting at 11,820,000 yen), and the GT2 went up to 23,720,000 yen; the strict GT3 was 14,190,000 yen at this time, while the RS version commanded 16,800,000 yen. The newcomers to the 911 line-up, the Carrera 4S Cabriolet and the Turbo Cabriolet, were priced at 14,220,000 yen and 19,200,000 yen respectively.

2004 racing ... and rallying
The FIA GT Championship was a toss-up between Ferrari, Saleen and Maserati (Ferrari ultimately won the day), but there was no doubt about which manufacturer was the dominant force in the N-GT category – Porsche, with Lucas Luhr and Sascha Maassen sharing the drivers' title.

Porsche was also strong in the newly-formed Le Mans Endurance Series, taking three of the four 1000km races. There was also a Class win

of Tiptronic S transmission on most of these, plus the $89,800 '40 Jahre' model, and there was obviously plenty to keep the 911 enthusiast awake at night trying to figure out which one to buy.

The list of extras was staggering, and there were also engine upgrades to consider. In addition to the regular $13,990 X51 kit for the Carrera, or the $17,880 X50 version for the Turbo, there was a Performance Plus package for the turbocharged car. Priced at $29,280, it included the X50 kit, the X54 exhaust (with dual pipes on each side), ceramic brakes, Sport Techno alloys, and the newly introduced, thicker rimmed steering wheel.

It's fair to say, however, that American journalist, R J Garbosky, wasn't that impressed with the C4S Cabriolet, stating: "The top has the unique ability to operate at any speed up to 30mph for dramatic traffic action. This was super cool for the posing roll, but regrettably, the deep

delivered through the rear wheels, it was perhaps less suited to rallying than the earlier 911s, but it was an interesting motorsport excursion nonetheless.

A 2005 model year preview

The 2004 British Motor Show was held in late May at the NEC, with Porsche occupying stand 320 in Hall 6. As the press release noted: "We will be showcasing our full GT line-up, led by the outstanding 612bhp Porsche Carrera GT supercar. In support will be the 911 GT2, 911 GT3 and 911 GT3RS, and a 911 GT3 Cup racing car. In total, there will be nine Porsche 911 models on display, including the new 911 Turbo S that is making its world premiere at Birmingham.

"The new Porsche 911 Turbo S builds on the awe-inspiring attributes of the 911 Turbo, and takes the driving experience to a new, higher level. The Turbo S, which is available both as a coupé and convertible, is based on the current 996 generation 911 Turbo and will join the broadest ever range of 911 models when it goes on sale in August.

"The evocative twin-turbocharged, 3.6-litre flat six engine has been tuned in the Turbo S model to develop more power and torque for even greater performance – and Porsche engineers have achieved this while ensuring fuel consumption and emissions barely differ from the standard Turbo model.

"The vital statistics of the Turbo S are impressive. Power is raised by 30bhp to 450bhp, and pulling power leaps to 457lbft from 413lbft. This increase in engine responsiveness manifests itself particularly during in-gear acceleration – which is stunning. The engine delivers these remarkable figures courtesy of larger turbochargers, modified intercoolers and revised engine management electronics. Additionally, the six-speed manual transmission has been strengthened to handle the torque increase.

"The brakes of the 911 Turbo S have also been uprated similarly. Fitted as standard are the Porsche Ceramic Composite Brake (PCCB) system,

The GT3 has proved very popular in Japan, despite the official national speed limit being relatively low.

(tenth overall) at the 24-hour classic that lent its name to the series, and the ALMS races on the other side of the Atlantic also proved to be a happy hunting ground for the 911s, the Alex Job Racing equipe taking the honours at the end of the season.

Wolf Henzler was runaway winner of the 2004 Porsche Supercup.

The car used in the series was little changed, incidentally, with only minor interior modifications and safety enhancements.

The end of 2004 saw a return of Porsche's flat-six to the rallying arena when the 911 GT3 was campaigned by the Belgian Future World team. With the car's sheer size and 381bhp being

The 40th Anniversary 911 on display at Makuhari Messe, and its special tail badge (below). This desirable model, which will doubtless be a collector's item one day, sold for 12,620,000 yen in Japan.

Below: Family Garage in Chiba City (the author's local official Porsche dealer), with a GT3 at the front of the showroom.

offering a 50% weight reduction per wheel over the conventional steel brake disc equivalent, as well as superior fade resistance characteristics under heavy braking.

"Taking the performance potential of the Turbo S coupé and adding the versatility of an electric folding roof, the £105,030 Turbo S Cabriolet is the ultimate expression of open-top 911 motoring. Roof operation is electro-hydraulic and allows the driver to open or close the roof fully automatically in just 20 seconds at the touch of a button. And to allow even greater flexibility, the driver can choose to lower or close the roof either at a standstill, or at speeds of up to 31mph (50kph). Like all Porsche 911 Cabriolet models, the Turbo S also comes as standard with a removable aluminium hardtop – weighing only 33kg (73lb) – for year-round convenience.

"The Turbo S Cabriolet shares the same 450bhp engine as the £99,300 coupé, and has a six-speed manual gearbox. However, both the coupé and convertible Turbo S models can be ordered with the Porsche Tiptronic S five-speed automatic transmission.

"Standard equipment on the Turbo S includes metallic paint (including a special colour – Dark Olive Metallic), Xenon headlights, a Bose audio system, and the Porsche Communication Management System (PCM) incorporating audio, telephone and satellite navigation functionality. Additionally, the Turbo S offers 18-inch alloy wheels painted in GT Silver Metallic, plus full leather interior trim, aluminium-coloured instrument dials, cruise control and a CD autochanger."

The Turbo S powerplant was actually nothing new, as it was simply the adoption of the X50 option. The M96/70E produced 450bhp DIN at 5700rpm, and 457lbft of torque at 3500rpm. Turbo S variants officially weighed the same as the equivalent regular Turbo models.

It was announced at this time that Valmet was to cut Boxster production to around 50 cars per day for the 2005 model year (circa 11,000 units per annum), while Zuffenhausen was to reduce production by around 20 per cent. The Stuttgart-built 911 would

The €279,000 GT3 RSR was introduced in readiness for the 2004 season. The bulging wheelarches allowed wider tyres to be fitted to make the most of the car's suspension revisions, while the 3.6 litre NA flat-six (developing 445bhp and 299lbft of torque) was linked to a six-speed sequential gearbox.

remain at a level of about 150 cars per day, but a cut in overtime and longer holidays were introduced in order to reduce overall production levels.

New Porsche 911 revealed

Just before the 2004 British Motor Show, PCGB released preliminary details of the new 911. The text read as follows: "This latest generation (Type 997) builds on the proven strengths of the 911 model line to move the evolution of the iconic sports coupé on another stage. The established design cues that have made the Porsche 911 recognizable the world over are given new energy, and further changes under the skin provide increased efficiency, more safety and greater levels of driving enjoyment.

"Two new 911 models will be launched simultaneously: The 911 Carrera with a 325bhp, 3.6-litre six-cylinder 'boxer' engine, and the 911 Carrera S, powered by a newly-developed 3.8-litre engine, which delivers 355bhp. With torque output of 295lbft, the S model accelerates from zero to 100kph (0-62mph) in 4.8 seconds. The Carrera achieves this in exactly five seconds. Top speeds for the Carrera and Carrera S are 177mph (285kph) and 182mph (293kph) respectively.

"Both 911 models have a newly-developed six-speed manual gearbox and revised chassis dynamics, which includes active suspension, called Porsche Active Suspension Management (PASM). In the 'normal' position, PASM provides a sporty and comfortable balance to the suspension. Engaging the 'sport' function, however, makes the suspension firmer, providing enhanced agility for enthusiastic drivers. PASM is fitted as standard on the S model and available as an option on the Carrera. A further option for both models is a sports suspension package, which lowers the body by 20mm, offered in combination with a mechanical limited-slip differential.

"The specification of the wheels and tyres fitted to the Porsche 911 has also evolved: The 911 Carrera now has, as standard, 8J x 18 wheels with 235/40 ZR18 tyres at the front and

A GT3RS running in the 2004 ALMS series in the States.

Action from the 2004 Carrera Cup Asia, which was launched as a new series in the previous year.

10J x 18 wheels with 265/40 ZR18 tyres at the rear. For the first time, 19-inch diameter wheels are available on the Porsche 911 and the Carrera S is equipped with 8J x 19 wheels with 235/35 ZR19 tyres (front) and 11J x 19 wheels with 295/30 ZR19 tyres (rear).

"The design of the latest Porsche 911 is a logical continuation of the 911 story, now in its 41st year. The result of the new exterior design – including a wider track and more emphasis on the waist – is a 911 which is even more dynamic, clear, powerful and, at the same time, elegant. Other features of the evolutionary design are new circular headlamps, more prominent bumpers and wheelarches, dual-arm exterior mirrors, altered seam characteristics and a more aerodynamic rear spoiler.

"The price for the new Porsche 911 Carrera is £58,380 and £65,000 for the 911 Carrera S. Both models offer Porsche Stability Management (PSM) fitted as standard. These prices also include UK specification feature content including full leather interior trim and graduated tinted windscreen.

"The new 997 generation Porsche 911 is being introduced only as a two-wheel drive Carrera model. The current line-up of wide-bodied all-wheel drive models (Carrera 4, Carrera 4S, Turbo) plus GT2, GT3 and GT3RS, will continue in production.

"The new 911 models will be launched across continental Europe on 17 July and will go on sale throughout the UK from 18 September. The car will make its world motor show debut at the Paris Salon in September."

The new Carrera engine had the same bore and stroke (and therefore capacity) as the 996 model, but fine-tuning of the intake tracts and other minor revisions allowed the engineers at Weissach to extract an extra 5bhp. In its latest guise, the 3.6-litre engine developed 325bhp DIN at 6800rpm, and 273lbft of torque at 4250rpm.

The Carrera S had a bore and stroke measurement of 99 x 82.8mm, the increase on the bore giving 3824cc, and calling for new pistons and so on, while other modifications included a revised intake manifold design. The twin exhausts of the S model gave the car a purposeful look, hinting at the 355bhp DIN available at 6600rpm, and the 295lbft of torque developed at 4600rpm.

The redesigned body was a touch wider and a great deal more shapely around the rear flanks. The

The tail, interior, and a couple of detail shots of the Turbo S, seen here in drophead guise. The Turbo S had an elegant silver badge on the rear panel, with the 'S' suffix giving a subtle clue as to what lay beneath the engine cover.

fresh interior was also welcome, but the big news concerned the new headlight arrangement. The return to a traditional Porsche front mask was a good idea; one Japanese dealer told the author that many buyers had a problem with the early 996, as it looked so similar to the Boxster. Even after the 2002 facelift, people were still asking for a more distinctive 911 face. Doubtless, the feeling was much the same all over the world.

On the subject of design, Harm Lagaay, Porsche's head of styling, retired on 1 July 2004, handing the reins to Michael Mauer. Mauer was born in Germany in 1962, and had a sparkling career at Mercedes-Benz before moving to Saab in the year 2000. But, like Tony Lapine before him, Lagaay would be sorely missed.

As Wendelin Wiedeking said after the announcement: "Porsche owes a lot to Harm Lagaay. His design philosophy and skill have made a major contribution to the high standing of the 911, Boxster and Cayenne in all world markets and therefore to the success of the company as a whole. He is entitled to be proud of his work."

Swansong
Although it was not launched at any of the motor shows until the Paris Salon opened its gates to the public on 25 September, the details of the 997 were already known long before the 2005 model year line-up was announced. The newly-introduced Turbo S would, of course, have its place guaranteed, while the regular 996 Carrera coupé had a definite replacement. It was the other mix that was the unknown quantity, especially with the higher-powered Carrera S in the equation.

As it happens, things followed a fairly established path, at least in Germany and other parts of Europe. Alongside the new 911 coupé models there was a 996 Targa (€82,275), 996 Carrera Cabriolet (€84,480), a 996 C4S (€89,815), 996 C4S Cabriolet (€99,792), a 996 Turbo (€128,675), a 996 Turbo Cabriolet (€138,652), a 996 Turbo S (€142,248), a 996 Turbo S Cabriolet (€152,225), a 996 GT3 (€102,112) and a 996 GT2 (€184,675), this in amongst a Porsche line-up that ranged in price from €42,255 for the cheapest Boxster, all the way up to €452,690 for the Carrera GT.

christophorus **308**

The Porsche Magazine

June/July 2004

Driving
With the Cayenne through the Australian wilderness

Fascination
The Carrera GT tours Germany in a glass case

Premiere
The new 911 Carrera is here

Cover of the legendary Christophorus magazine – Porsche's in-house publication – announcing the arrival of the face-lifted, 2005 model year 911 Carrera.

Naturally, as other 997 variants were introduced, certain 996 models were dropped, while others simply fell by the wayside to ensure that the 911 line-up for the 2006 model year was entirely 997-based.

Meanwhile, turnover and profits were up again in Stuttgart, and Wiedeking reported expected sales in excess of 80,000 units at the company's AGM in January 2005, this

forecast being delivered despite record unemployment in Germany and continuing fears over rising oil prices. Still, at least Porsche fans were able to celebrate the arrival of the latest 997 Cabriolet in the New Year.

The export markets
Naturally, the big news in the States was the debut of the 997 series, with sales having started on 28 August. The

Tiptronic S transmission was a $3420 extra.

After announcing record sales in the States for 2004 (33,289 units, including 10,227 911s), the Detroit Show played host to the launch of the 997 Cabriolet. This was actually the world debut of the drophead (probably a nod to the fact that the C4S Cabriolet was a huge hit in the States), the NAIAS event opening its doors to the press on 9 January, although, as elsewhere, sales didn't start until the spring. The Cabriolet body added a $9800 premium to the cost of the 3.6 or 3.8-litre base car.

At the end of 2005, PCNA celebrated another record sales year, moving 33,859 cars in North America, with the 911 accounting for 10,653 units – an increase of four per cent on the previous year.

The UK was rather like Germany, with a full line of 996 models augmenting the two new coupés. At the end of 2004, the 911 line-up, ranging in price from £58,380 to £126,640, including the 997 Carrera coupé, 997 Carrera S coupé, 996 Cabriolet, 996 Targa, the 996 C4S, Turbo and Turbo S grades in closed and open guise, the 996 GT3 and flagship 996 GT2.

By the summer, already the 997 models had started to expand, with the £72,230 Carrera S Cabriolet joining the PCGB catalogue, but all the other 996 cars remained in price lists as unsold stock had to be cleared. As 2005 drew to a close, however, only the turbocharged vehicles continued alongside the 997-series machines, which now included coupé and soft-top versions of the strict Carrera, Carrera S, Carrera 4 and C4S.

Meanwhile, *Autocar* carried out its traditional 0-100-0 test, which involves accelerating from standstill up to 100mph (160kph) and then coming to a complete stop again in the shortest possible distance. The Bugatti Veyron was the best production car, doing this in a remarkable 9.9 seconds, but the 911 Turbo wasn't far behind at 12.5 seconds. It was a fitting tribute to a

3.6-litre Carrera had a specification very similar to the old Carrera, with a sunroof, leather trim and automatic air conditioning included in the price, while 18-inch wheels were now the norm, along with the traction control system (including ABD, PCM and ASR) that was previously a $1235 option. Other bonuses were rain-sensing wipers and a HomeLink garage door opener.

Moving up to the Carrera S brought the 3.8-litre power-unit, a 19-inch wheel and tyre combination, the PASM active suspension, Bi-Xenon headlights, and a Sport steering wheel.

Having started with six 996s for 2005, the US price list for December 2004 was revised to include new Carrera variants alongside just three 996-based models – the $99,900 GT3, the $131,400 Turbo S coupé, and the $141,200 Turbo S Cabriolet. Compared to these prices, the strict Carrera coupé looked a snip at $69,300, and even the S version offered good value at $79,100; the

A rear three-quarter shot of the Type 997 Carrera, this car having the optional 19-inch wheels found on the Carrera S.

much-loved supercar about to fade into the history books.

Japan continued to provide Porsche with a useful market, with over 3000 vehicles finding new homes in the Land of the Rising Sun to set a new sales record for the country. Japan, too, carried over most of the 996s into 2005, with the new 10,460,000 yen Carrera and 12,480,000 yen Carrera S being joined by the old Carrera, Carrera 4, C4S, Turbo and Turbo S in tin-top and drophead form, plus the Targa, GT3 and GT2 – the latter the most expensive car in the 911 range at 26,061,000 yen. Most automatic models were supplied with right-hand drive, although the majority of variants were available with lhd or rhd.

As for Australia, the $195,225 997 Carrera and $221,100 Carrera S (an automatic transmission added $8000 in both cases) were kept company by the old Carrera coupé, Cabriolet and Targa, the C4S coupé and convertible, the Turbo coupé and convertible, and the GT3 and GT3RS. The original coupé was the cheapest of the bunch at $187,600, while the Turbo Cabriolet was a hefty $345,500

– well over twice the price of a Lexus SC430, or the cost of a Mercedes C55 AMG and a CLK500 Cabriolet put together!

By the middle of the year, the last of the 996 Carrera coupés had gone, but the other vehicles soldiered on for a while longer. As 2005 gave way to 2006, though, only the Turbo coupé, Turbo Cabriolet, GT3 and GT3RS remained on the books, and these were gone long before the midway point in the following year.

2005 racing review

The FIA GT Championship was dominated by Italian marques in the GT1 category (an epic battle between Ferrari and Maserati unfolded), but nothing could touch Porsche in GT2 – the Gruppe M Racing 911 GT3 RSR came out ahead by a huge margin in the end, ably driven by Marc Lieb and Mike Rockenfeller.

The Le Mans Endurance Series was extended to five rounds, though the new addition was Istanbul rather than Le Mans itself. Zytek and Pescarolo machines fought off the Audi challenge in the top category, while the GT2 category went to

With the retirement of Harm Lagaay, Michael Mauer became the new head of styling at Porsche in the summer of 2004. The 997 was therefore Lagaay's last major project.

The Turbo S, seen here in coupé and drophead guise, was one of the last 996s to soldier on into 2005.

The Sebah Automotive GT3 RSR that won the GT2 category in the 2005 Le Mans Endurance Series.

Porsche, thanks to the efforts of Sebah Automotive and its drivers, Marc Lieb and Xavier Pompidou.

The actual Le Mans 24-hour classic was almost a repeat of 2004, with the Audi R8 dominating, except that a Pescarolo-Judd managed to steal a place on the podium this time around. GT1 went to Chevrolet, but the first seven places in GT2 went to 911 drivers, led home by the Rockenfeller/ Lieb/Hindery car from the Alex Job Racing stable in tenth place.

The ALMS races were still very much Audi property, although the MG-Lolas gave the German manufacturer a run for its money in a couple of races. As much as Audi owned the LMP1 category, GT2 belonged to Porsche. This year, the Alex Job Racing boys had to bow to the Petersen Motorsports/White Lightning Racing equipe, fielding Jorg Bergmeister, Patrick Long and Lucas Luhr as their drivers. With the victorious debut of the RS Spyder at Laguna Seca, Porsche fans had something to cheer for in LMP2, too, in the future.

The GT2 winner at Le Mans was this Alex Job Racing car, driven by Mike Rockenfeller, Marc Lieb and Leo Hindery.

The Grand-Am Championship suddenly came alive, with more rounds, each attracting larger fields. Daytona was still the big event of the Grand-Am season, and the Porsche-powered Brumos Fabcar finished eighth, two places ahead of the GT Class-winning 911. It was a similar story in most of the other races, with the Fabcar finishing in the middle of the DP competitors, although BMW and Pontiac did a good job of preventing the 911 GT3 from taking the GT silverware on far too many occasions in 2005.

Action from the Sebring 12-hour Race, which was part of the ALMS series. The number 23 car was one of the Alex Job Racing machines that failed to finish, number 31 came seventh (first in Class) thanks to Jorg Bergmeister, Patrick Long and Lucas Luhr, and TRG's number 66 car (seen here being chased by another 911) finished 16th overall.

Action from the 24-hour race held at the Nürburgring – an event that always attracts a huge Porsche following.

Marc Duez trying to tame GT3 power in the 2005 Ardenne Bleue Rally. The Duez/ Muth pairing finished 15th overall, and first in the GT-N Class.

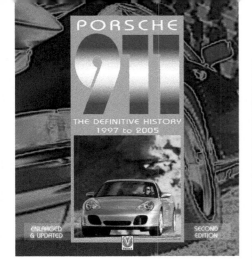

Appendix I

Year-by-year range details

Here are the brief specifications of all the 996-type Porsches, arranged in chronological and engine size order. Column one shows the model, the second column carries engine details (to be used in conjunction with Appendix II), while the third contains any other useful notes. Only production road cars are listed for each model year. Therefore, prototypes and pure racing variants are not shown:

1998

Carrera Coupé	M96/01 (3.4)	
Carrera Cabriolet	M96/01 (3.4)	From March 1998

1999

Carrera Coupé	M96/01 (3.4)	
Carrera Cabriolet	M96/01 (3.4)	
Carrera 4 Coupé	M96/02 (3.4)	
Carrera 4 Cabriolet	M96/02 (3.4)	

2000

Carrera Coupé	M96/04 (3.4)	
Carrera Cabriolet	M96/04 (3.4)	
Carrera 4 Coupé	M96/04 (3.4)	
Carrera 4 Cabriolet	M96/04 (3.4)	
GT3	M96/76 (3.6)	From March 1999

2001

Carrera Coupé	M96/04 (3.4)	
Carrera Cabriolet	M96/04 (3.4)	
Carrera 4 Coupé	M96/04 (3.4)	
Carrera 4 Cabriolet	M96/04 (3.4)	
GT2	M96/70S (3.6)	From January 2001
GT3	M96/76 (3.6)	
Turbo Coupé	M96/70 (3.6)	From March 2000

2002

Carrera Coupé	M96/03 (3.6)	
Carrera Cabriolet	M96/03 (3.6)	
Carrera Targa	M96/03 (3.6)	
Carrera 4 Coupé	M96/03 (3.6)	
Carrera 4 Cabriolet	M96/03 (3.6)	
Carrera 4S Coupé	M96/03 (3.6)	
GT2	M96/70S (3.6)	
Turbo Coupé	M96/70 (3.6)	

2003

Carrera Coupé	M96/03 (3.6)	
Carrera Cabriolet	M96/03 (3.6)	
Carrera Targa	M96/03 (3.6)	
Carrera 4 Coupé	M96/03 (3.6)	
Carrera 4 Cabriolet	M96/03 (3.6)	
Carrera 4S Coupé	M96/03 (3.6)	
GT2	M96/70S (3.6)	
Turbo Coupé	M96/70 (3.6)	

continues overleaf

	2004	
Carrera Coupé	M96/03 (3.6)	
Carrera Cabriolet	M96/03 (3.6)	
Carrera Targa	M96/03 (3.6)	
Carrera 4 Coupé	M96/03 (3.6)	
Carrera 4 Cabriolet	M96/03 (3.6)	
Carrera 4S Coupé	M96/03 (3.6)	
Carrera 4S Cabriolet	M96/03 (3.6)	
GT2	M96/70SL (3.6)	
GT3	M96/79 (3.6)	From March 2003
GT3RS	M96/79 (3.6)	
Turbo Coupé	M96/70 (3.6)	
Turbo Cabriolet	M96/70 (3.6)	
	2005	
Carrera Cabriolet	M96/03 (3.6)	To March 2005
Carrera Targa	M96/03 (3.6)	
Carrera 4 Coupé	M96/03 (3.6)	
Carrera 4 Cabriolet	M96/03 (3.6)	
Carrera 4S Coupé	M96/03 (3.6)	
Carrera 4S Cabriolet	M96/03 (3.6)	
GT2	M96/70SL (3.6)	
GT3	M96/79 (3.6)	
GT3RS	M96/79 (3.6)	
Turbo Coupé	M96/70 (3.6)	
Turbo Cabriolet	M96/70 (3.6)	
Turbo S Coupé	M96/70E (3.6)	From August 2004
Turbo S Cabriolet	M96/70E (3.6)	From August 2004

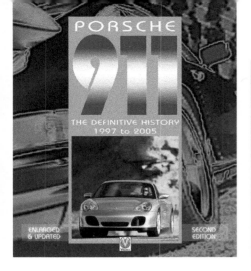

Appendix II
Engine specifications

A survey of all the engines employed in the 996 series, complete with the leading specifications, major changes and any other notes of interest. Only power-units employed in production road cars are covered by this appendix:

Type M96/01
Production (MY) 1998-1999
Cylinders .... Six, water-cooled
Main bearings......................... Seven
Valve operation...................... Dohc per bank
Bore & stroke .... 96 x 78mm
Cubic capacity 3387cc
Compression ratio.................. 11.3:1
Fuel system .... Fuel-injection
Hp @ rpm .... 300bhp DIN @ 6800
Torque @ rpm .... 258lbft @ 4600
Serial numbers .... 66W 00501- & 66X 00501-

Notes: Used in the early 996s (MT & AT). The X51 option brought an uprated engine, giving 320bhp and 265lbft.

Type M96/02
Production (MY) 1999
Specifications .... As per Type M96/01
Serial numbers 68X 00501-

Notes: Used in the early Carrera 4s (MT & AT).

Type M96/03
Production (MY) 2002-2005
Cylinders .... Six, water-cooled
Main bearings......................... Seven
Valve operation...................... Dohc per bank
Bore & stroke .... 96 x 82.8mm
Cubic capacity 3596cc
Compression ratio.................. 11.3:1
Fuel system .... Fuel-injection
Hp @ rpm .... 320bhp DIN @ 6800
Torque @ rpm .... 273lbft @ 4250
Serial numbers 662 00501-, 663 00501-, 664 00501-
.... & 665 00501-

Notes: Used in the face-lifted Carreras (MT & AT). The X51 option brought an uprated engine, giving 345bhp and 273lbft.

Type M96/04
Production (MY) 2000-2001
Specifications .... As per Type M96/01
Serial numbers .... 66Y 00501- & 661 00501-

Notes: Used in the 2000 and 2001 MY Carrera models (MT & AT). The X51 option brought an uprated engine, giving 320bhp and 265lbft.

continues overleaf

Type M96/70

Production (MY)	2001-2005
Cylinders	Six, water-cooled
Main bearings	Seven plus one outrigger
Valve operation	Dohc per bank
Bore & stroke	100 x 76.4mm
Cubic capacity	3600cc
Compression ratio	9.4:1
Fuel system	Fuel-injection
Hp @ rpm	420bhp DIN @ 6000
Torque @ rpm	413lbft @ 2700
Serial numbers	641 00501-, 642 00501-, 643 00501-, 644 00501- & 645 00501-

Notes; Used in the series Turbo models (MT & AT), built from March 2000 (classed as an early 2001 model). The GT2 used the M96/70S engine, which developed 462bhp and 457lbft of torque (or 483bhp in its later M96/70SL guise), while the X50 option of an uprated 450bhp/457lbft Turbo engine was designated the M96/70E.

Type M96/76

Production (MY)	2000-2001
Cylinders	Six, water-cooled
Main bearings	Seven plus one outrigger
Valve operation	Dohc per bank
Bore & stroke	100 x 76.4mm
Cubic capacity	3600cc
Compression ratio	11.7:1
Fuel system	Fuel-injection
Hp @ rpm	360bhp DIN @ 7200
Torque @ rpm	273lbft @ 5000
Serial numbers	63Y 21501- & 631 21501-

Notes: Used in the limited production GT3, built from March 1999 (classed as an early 2000 model).

Type M96/79

Production (MY)	2004-2005
Cylinders	Six, water-cooled
Main bearings	Seven plus one outrigger
Valve operation	Dohc per bank
Bore & stroke	100 x 76.4mm
Cubic capacity	3600cc
Compression ratio	11.7:1
Fuel system	Fuel-injection
Hp @ rpm	381bhp DIN @ 7400
Torque @ rpm	284lbft @ 5000
Serial numbers	634 24501- & 635 24501-

Notes: Used in the series production GT3 (classed as an early 2004 model). The GT3RS used the same basic unit, but was given a different batch of serial numbers (starting at 26501 instead of 24501).

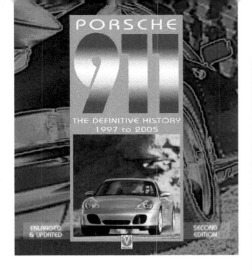

Appendix III

Chassis numbers & production figures

Please note that the following blocks of numbers are the start numbers for each of the model year production runs. Production figures are shown at the end of this appendix:

W-Serie models

1998 MY	Carrera Coupé	WP0ZZZ99ZWS 600061-
	Carrera Coupé (USA)	WP0AA299ZWS 620061-
	Carrera Coupé (Brazil)	WP0ZZZ99ZWS 629801-
	Carrera Cabriolet	WP0ZZZ99ZWS 640061-
	Carrera Cabriolet (USA)	WP0CA299ZWS 650061-

Note: The 'USA' entry includes Canada and Mexico.

X-Serie models

1999 MY	Carrera & C4 Coupé	WP0ZZZ99ZXS 600061-
	Carrera & C4 Coupé (USA)	WP0AA299ZXS 620061-
	Carrera & C4 Coupé (Brazil)	WP0ZZZ99ZXS 629401-
	Carrera & C4 Cabriolet	WP0ZZZ99ZXS 640061-
	Carrera & C4 Cabriolet (USA)	WP0CA299ZXS 650061-
	Carrera & C4 Cabriolet (Brazil)	WP0ZZZ99ZXS 659601-

Y-Serie models

2000 MY	Carrera & C4 Coupé	WP0ZZZ99ZYS 600061-
	Carrera & C4 Coupé (USA)	WP0AA299ZYS 620061-
	Carrera & C4 Cabriolet	WP0ZZZ99ZYS 640061-
	Carrera & C4 Cabriolet (USA)	WP0CA299ZYS 650061-
	GT3	WP0ZZZ99ZYS 690061-

Note: The 'USA' entry now includes Canada, Mexico and Brazil.

1-Serie models

2001 MY	Carrera & C4 Coupé	WP0ZZZ99Z1S 600061-
	Carrera & C4 Coupé (USA)	WP0AA299Z1S 620061-
	Carrera & C4 Cabriolet	WP0ZZZ99Z1S 640061-
	Carrera & C4 Cabriolet (USA)	WP0CA299Z1S 650061-
	Turbo Coupé	WP0ZZZ99Z1S 680061-
	Turbo Coupé (USA)	WP0AA299Z1S 685061-
	GT3	WP0ZZZ99Z1S 690061-
	GT2	WP0ZZZ99Z1S 695061-

2-Serie models

2002 MY	Carrera, C4 & C4S Coupé	WP0ZZZ99Z2S 600061-
	Carrera, C4 & C4S Coupé (USA)	WP0AA299Z2S 620061-
	Carrera Targa	WP0ZZZ99Z2S 630061-
	Carrera Targa (USA)	WP0BA299Z2S 635061-
	Carrera & C4 Cabriolet	WP0ZZZ99Z2S 640061-
	Carrera & C4 Cabriolet (USA)	WP0CA299Z2S 650061-
	Turbo Coupé	WP0ZZZ99Z2S 680061-
	Turbo Coupé (USA)	WP0AA299Z2S 685061-
	GT2	WP0ZZZ99Z2S 695061-
	GT2 (USA)	WP0AA299Z2S 696061-

3-Serie models

2003 MY	Carrera, C4 & C4S Coupé	WP0ZZZ99Z3S 600061-
	Carrera, C4 & C4S Coupé (USA)	WP0AA299Z3S 620061-
	Carrera Targa	WP0ZZZ99Z3S 630061-
	Carrera Targa (USA)	WP0BA299Z3S 635061-
	Carrera & C4 Cabriolet	WP0ZZZ99Z3S 640061-

continues overleaf

Carrera & C4 Cabriolet (USA)	WP0CA299Z3S 650061-
Turbo Coupé	WP0ZZZ99Z3S 680061-
Turbo Coupé (USA)	WP0AA299Z3S 685061-
GT2	WP0ZZZ99Z3S 695061-
GT2 (USA)	WP0AA299Z3S 696061-

4-Serie models

2004 MY	Carrera, C4 & C4S Coupé	WP0ZZZ99Z4S 600061-
	Carrera, C4 & C4S Coupé (USA)	WP0AA299Z4S 620061-
	Carrera Targa	WP0ZZZ99Z4S 630061-
	Carrera Targa (USA)	WP0BA299Z4S 635061-
	Carrera, C4 & C4S Cabriolet	WP0ZZZ99Z4S 640061-
	Carrera, C4 & C4S Cabrio. (USA)	WP0CA299Z4S 650061-
	Turbo Cabriolet	WP0ZZZ99Z4S 670061-
	Turbo Cabriolet (USA)	WP0CA299Z4S 675061-
	Turbo Coupé	WP0ZZZ99Z4S 680061-
	Turbo Coupé (USA)	WP0AA299Z4S 685061-
	GT3 & GT3RS	WP0ZZZ99Z4S 690061-
	GT3 (USA)	WP0AA299Z4S 692061-
	GT2	WP0ZZZ99Z4S 695061-
	GT2 (USA)	WP0AA299Z4S 696061-

5-Serie models

2005 MY	Carrera 4 & C4S Coupé	WP0ZZZ99Z5S 600061-
	Carrera 4 & C4S Coupé (USA)	WP0AA299Z5S 620061-
	Carrera Targa	WP0ZZZ99Z5S 630061-
	Carrera Targa (USA)	WP0BA299Z5S 635061-
	Carrera, C4 & C4S Cabriolet	WP0ZZZ99Z5S 640061-
	Carrera, C4 & C4S Cabrio. (USA)	WP0CA299Z5S 650061-
	Turbo, Turbo S Cabriolet	WP0ZZZ99Z5S 670061-
	Turbo, Turbo S Cabriolet (USA)	WP0CA299Z5S 675061-
	Turbo, Turbo S Coupé	WP0ZZZ99Z5S 680061-
	Turbo, Turbo S Coupé (USA)	WP0AA299Z5S 685061-
	GT3 & GT3RS	WP0ZZZ99Z5S 690061-
	GT3 (USA)	WP0AA299Z5S 692061-
	GT2	WP0ZZZ99Z5S 695061-
	GT2 (USA)	WP0AA299Z5S 696061-

Production figures

Please note that these annual figures do not include the pure racing cars, or the Carrera Cup competition cars. The 911 column includes all normally-aspirated 911 variants; turbocharged cars are in the second column. Incidentally, while the early entries are accurate, being those logged with the German VDA, the 2004 CY figures include the first batch of 997 models. It is also possible that a handful of turbocharged cars (as well as a few niche market NA models) were built in 2005, so the last entry and final total is therefore for guidance only:

	NA 911s	Turbos	Total	Cumulative total
1997 CY	1766	–	1766	1766
1998 CY	19,313	–	19,313	21,079
1999 CY	22,621	–	22,621	43,700
2000 CY	20,923	3591	24,514	68,214
2001 CY	23,038	6340	29,378	97,592
2002 CY	27,083	6290	33,373	130,965
2003 CY	22,128	4083	26,211	157,176
2004 CY	24,388	4634	29,022	186,198

Total water-cooled cars (1997 to the end of 2004)   186,198

The Essential Buyer's Guides

Having these books in your pocket is just like having a real marque expert by your side. Benefit from the authors' experience, learn how to spot a bad car quickly, and how to assess a promising one like a professional. Get the right car at the right price!
Over 100 titles now available in this series!

Paperback • 19.5x13.9cm • 64 pages • full colour illustration

Other books in this series: *Porsche 911 – The Definitive History*

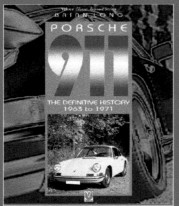

ISBN: 978-1-787115-40-8

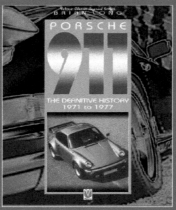

ISBN: 978-1-787115-41-5

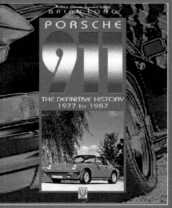

ISBN: 978-1-787115-42-2

ISBN: 978-1-787115-43-9

Volumes 1-4 available in print and eBook formats

For further details, or to browse Veloce's entire eBook range, please visit:

http://digital.veloce.co.uk

· ·

The 6th book in the series (2004-2012)

This book – the sixth volume in the series – continues the definitive history of the hugely successful 997-series, with in-depth detail on all the road cars sold around the world, as well as the 997's competition exploits.

ISBN: 978-1-845848-64-4
Hardback • 25x20.7cm
• 208 pages • 363 pictures

For more information on Veloce titles, please visit our website at
www.veloce.co.uk
• email: info@veloce.co.uk

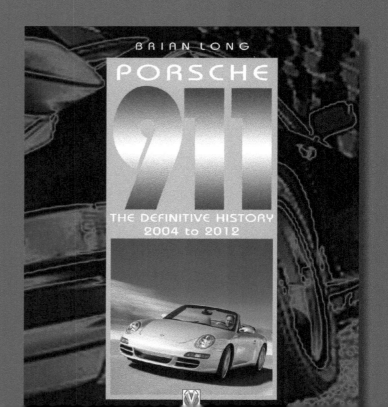

INDEX

The Porsche company, its products and subsidiaries are mentioned throughout the book.